STUDENT UNIT GUIDE

A2 Psychology
UNIT 5

Edexcel

Applications of Psychology and Research Methods

Christine Brain

Philip Allan Updates
Market Place
Deddington
Oxfordshire
OX15 0SE

tel: 01869 338652
fax: 01869 337590
e-mail: sales@philipallan.co.uk
www.philipallan.co.uk

ISBN-13: 978-0-86003-888-7
ISBN-10: 0-86003-888-2

This Guide has been written specifically to support students preparing for the Edexcel A2 Psychology Unit 5 examination. The content has been neither approved nor endorsed by Edexcel and remains the sole responsibility of the author.

Printed by MPG Books, Bodmin

Environmental information
The paper on which this title is printed is sourced from managed, sustainable forests.

P00727

Contents

Introduction

About this guide

This is a guide to Unit 5 of the Edexcel A2 specification: Applications of Psychology and Research Methods.

Aims

The aim of this guide is to provide you with a clear understanding of the requirements of Unit 5 of the A2 specification and to advise you on how best to meet these requirements.

This guide looks at:

- the psychology you need to know about
- what you need to be able to do and what skills you need
- how you could go about learning the necessary material
- what is being examined
- what you should expect in the examination
- how you could tackle the different styles of exam question
- the format of the exam, including what questions might look like
- how questions are marked, including examples of answers, with examiner's comments

It is not a textbook — there is no substitute for reading the required material and taking notes — and it does not tell you the actual questions on your paper, or give you the answers!

Study skills and revision strategies

If you have been studying the Unit 5 material on one of the three applications (child, environmental or health psychology) and research methods, and have engaged in a reasonable amount of learning up to now, you can make good use of this guide.

This guide can also help if you know very little of the material and have only a short time before the examination. If this describes you, you have a lot of work and long hours of study ahead — but you can do it.

Revision plan

- Start at least 4 weeks before the exam date (sooner if possible).
- Using times that suit you (6 a.m. might be a great time to study!), draw up a blank timetable for each of the weeks.

- On the timetable, fill in all your urgent commitments (cancel as many plans as you can).
- Divide up what is left, allocating slots to all your subjects as appropriate. Don't forget to build in meal times, breaks and time for sleep.
- Stick to the plan if at all possible, but if you have to, amend it as you go.
- When studying, have frequent, short rests and no distractions.

Examination structure and skills

Unit 5 is divided into two parts. One part consists of three applications of psychology: child, environmental and health. You must select one of these applications. The other part of Unit 5 focuses on research methods.

Assessment Objectives

The Assessment Objectives are listed in the specification. A brief explanation is given below, but check the full list of what you will be assessed on.

Assessment Objective 1 (AO1): knowledge and understanding

- You need to show your knowledge and understanding of psychological terminology and concepts through appropriate use and application.
- You must demonstrate knowledge and understanding of psychological theories, studies, methods and concepts, as well as psychological principles, perspectives and applications.
- You must communicate clearly and effectively, and present and select material well.

Assessment Objective 2 (AO2): applications of knowledge and understanding, analysis, synthesis and evaluation

You must be able to:

- analyse and evaluate psychological theories and concepts, referring to relevant evidence
- appraise psychological studies and methods

Assessment Objective 3 (AO3): experiment and investigation

This is examined in Unit 5 within the research methods questions. It involves planning and conducting research.

The Unit 5 exam

Unit 5 is assessed in a 90-minute exam. A total of 72 marks are available. This means you need to score around 1 mark per minute, with 18 minutes to spare for reading and thinking. There are two sections: the first includes questions on Research Methods, for 36 marks; the other includes the three Applications. You have to answer questions on one application, also for 36 marks. In general, you can expect to gain a

mark for each point that answers the question, or for elaboration of a point. Answers must be communicated 'clearly and effectively' (see AO1 above). Avoid one-word answers unless they are asked for.

Some Unit 5 papers require you to write an essay at the end of each question, and some do not. You should be prepared to write an essay worth between 12 and 16 marks. Overall, each application has approximately 14/15 marks for knowledge and understanding (AO1) and approximately 22/21 marks for evaluation and comment (AO2).

Essay mark scheme

Essays have 2 marks (AO1 marks) available for clarity and communication (use of terms, spelling, ways of expressing points) and 2 marks (AO2 marks) for balance and breadth. In addition, for a 12-mark essay, you need to give four AO1 'knowledge and understanding' points and four AO2 'evaluation and comment' points. For a 14-mark essay, five AO1 points and five AO2 points are required. For a 16-mark essay, six AO1 points and six AO2 points are needed.

AO1 and AO2: getting it right

You must answer the question that is set — you should then cover the AO1 and AO2 skills. The key words in the question (called **injunctions**) are a guide to what you need to write. If you answer the question, you will automatically do what is required.

Table 1 shows some examples of how AO1 injunctions are used and Table 2 shows examples of AO2 injunctions. Note that it is not so much the word itself (e.g. 'describe') that makes it AO1 or AO2 as the whole question. The figures in brackets suggest the mark allocation you might expect for such a question.

Table 1 Examples of AO1 questions/injunctions

Type of question	What is being asked for
Describe a theory... (4)	Say what something is (a theory in this case); this could include an example. Imagine describing the theory to someone who knows little about it.
Identify a method... (1)	Give enough information so that the examiner can understand what is being referred to. For example, if asked to identify a method used by Ainsworth to look at attachment types, the answer might be 'the strange situation' (child psychology).
Name a type of play... (1)	Give a name or term. For example, if asked for a type of play, the answer might be 'solitary play' (child psychology).
Outline... (3)	Follow the instruction for describe, but remember that this injunction usually requires less detail, and hence carries fewer marks.
Describe a study... (5)	Try to give the aim of the study, the method, the results and the conclusion(s).

Table 2 Examples of AO2 questions/injunctions

Type of question	What is being asked for
Outline a strength of... (2)	You are asked to outline something, so the injunction seems to be AO1. However, because what is outlined is a strength (in this case), and in this way you are asked to evaluate something, this question would carry AO2 marks. Note, though, that you must still 'outline' (see Table 1).
Evaluate a study... (5)	Give comments, criticisms, good points and so on about a study. Consider strengths and weaknesses of the method, perhaps, or ethical issues raised. Look at alternative findings or consider whether justified conclusions are drawn.
Assess the evidence... (4)	Say what the evidence suggests and say how strong it is (e.g. the evidence for behaviour not being environmentally friendly — environmental psychology).

AO1 and AO2: injunctions in essay questions

Essay questions will always involve equal marks for AO1 and AO2. You should demonstrate knowledge and understanding and provide comment and evaluation. Remember spelling and use of terminology (2 AO1 marks for clarity and communication). Make sure you address all parts of the question (2 AO2 marks for breadth and balance). Table 3 shows the importance of knowing how AO1 and AO2 marks are split in each examination paper (excluding Unit 3, the coursework element, and the Research Methods part of Unit 5, which involves some AO3 marks).

Table 3 Approximate mark allocation AO1/AO2

	AO1	AO2	Total
AS Units 1 and 2	42	30	72
A2 Unit 4	28	44	72
A2 Unit 5 (Applications)	14	22	36
A2 Unit 6	36	36	72

Table 3 shows how, for the two AS units, you were assessed more on your knowledge and understanding (58%) than on your ability to comment and evaluate (42%). For Unit 4 you are assessed more on your ability to comment and evaluate (60%) than on your knowledge and understanding (40%). These approximate percentages are also true for the Applications question of Unit 5, although the other part of Unit 5 involves AO1, AO2 and AO3 and is, therefore, quite different. For Unit 6, your knowledge and understanding and your evaluation and comment skills are assessed equally.

Essentially, you have to learn material so you know and understand it, and then plan some criticisms, comments and evaluation points. As a rule of thumb, learn or plan as many evaluation and comment points as you learn information points.

Conclusions: use of injunctions and the AO1/AO2 split

Don't just think of a word in the question as being the whole question. For example, 'describe' is an AO1 command, but 'describe a strength...' is an AO2 injunction. 'Discuss' could signal AO2 marks if you are asked to 'discuss the usefulness of...' Because you are considering how useful something is, you are doing more than showing knowledge about it. The best approach is to *answer the question*.

Differences between AS and A2

Although a lot of what is true for AS still applies at A2 — for example, the AO1 and AO2 Assessment Objectives — the A2 exams require higher-level skills.

At A2, more marks are given for AO2 (evaluation and comment) than for AO1 (knowledge and understanding), except Unit 6, where both skills are assessed equally. This is quite different from AS. It means you need to comment, evaluate, assess, consider strengths and so on, more than you need to give information.

Greater depth is also required in your answers at A2. For example, you could be asked to consider the work of Oscar Newman and the concept of defensible space (environmental psychology). Psychology is built on evidence from studies, so when revising it is useful to have a list of names of studies and a brief outline of what each is about. Note also that half of Unit 5 is about Applications of Psychology, so be ready to apply your knowledge.

Content Guidance

Unit 5 is divided into two sections: Applications of Psychology and Research Methods.

Part (a): Applications of Psychology

You only need to study *one* of three applications:

- **(A) Child psychology**
  - Attachment
  - Deprivation and privation
  - Social development
- **(B) Environmental psychology**
  - Personal space and territoriality
  - Stress, crowding and urban living
  - Changing behaviour to save the environment
- **(C) Health psychology**
  - Health and substance abuse
  - Stress
  - Health promotion

Part (b): Research Methods

The material listed for Unit 3 must be covered, as well as the material listed for Unit 5 (part b). Unit 3 requires you to know about the main methods, including experiments, observations, questionnaires, interviews, case studies and content analysis, and you need to know advantages and disadvantages of each. You also need to know about ethical guidelines concerning the use of animals and humans in research. You need to know about designs (three participant designs and correlations) and sampling techniques. You need to demonstrate an understanding of: hypotheses; levels of measurement; validity; reliability; generalisability; counterbalancing; independent and dependent variables; situation and participant variables (and control of these); operationalisation of variables; selection of materials; and descriptive statistics.

In addition to the Unit 3 requirements, you will study material to do with inferential statistics. This includes: levels of significance; eight inferential tests; what one- and two-tailed means with regard to tests; standard deviation, variance and normal distribution; calculated and critical values; and how to decide whether the results of a test are significant or not. You must also know about analysis of qualitative data gathered by interview, observation or case study. Issues of subjectivity and objectivity are mentioned too.

This guide covers the compulsory Research Methods first, followed by the three Applications options. In the exam paper, however, the Applications questions come first.

Research methods

Ethical guidelines: human participants

You will have studied the British Psychological Society (BPS) guidelines for the use of humans in psychological research. The four guidelines named in the specification are outlined here. For Unit 5 you should be ready to name a guideline, outline what it involves, and be able to apply the idea in some way to a given situation.

Consent

The idea of consent ranges from simply asking participants if they are willing to take part in a psychology study to explaining exactly what will happen before asking if they are willing to take part. The more the detail of the study is explained, the more informed the consent is. In practice it is difficult to obtain informed consent because usually, if the participant knows all about the study, the results will be affected and will not be of any use.

So consent tends to mean that the participants have been told a bit about the study and have then been asked if they are willing to participate. They can be assured that they will be told all about the study at the end and at that stage they can withdraw their consent and ask for their results not to be included. However, this is not 'informed consent' so it is not ideal from an ethical point of view.

A study where informed consent was not obtained

Milgram (1963) could not get informed consent for his well-known study because the whole point was for the participant not to know that the person receiving the 'shocks' was an accomplice and that the shocks were not real. Milgram had to settle for a thorough debrief at the end of the study. He is criticised for not gaining a more informed consent.

A study where informed consent was obtained

Zimbardo (Haney et al., 1973) did get informed consent when he carried out his 'prisoner and guard' study. As the study was a simulation, he was able to tell the participants exactly what they would be doing. In this way his study was more ethical than Milgram's. The one thing he did not get consent for was the arresting that took place to get the 'prisoner' participants to the 'prison'. The participants were 'arrested' in front of their neighbours and underwent some humiliating procedures in a real police station before being driven to the mock prison. Zimbardo was criticised for this part of the study, even though he did obtain full consent for the rest of the research.

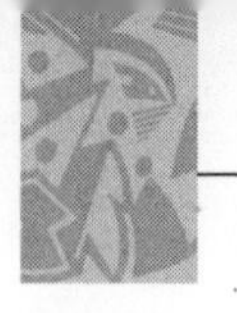

Confidentiality

Confidentiality is a guideline that is not too difficult to apply. Participants rarely have to be identified as part of a study. It is unusual for a participant to be identifiable, although there are exceptions. Names should never be used, and places can be changed to protect the identity of participants. Participants should be told that all results are confidential, and what will be done with the data should be transparent.

Where confidentiality is not maintained

It is easier than you think to reveal the identity of someone inadvertently. For example, if a case study is carried out at a private school and the area is mentioned, it is likely that there is only one such school in that area. If a teacher is then mentioned and perhaps linked to a specific subject, for example drama, then it is possible that there is only one drama teacher and that person is, therefore, easily identifiable. There must be careful attention to detail.

Confidentiality may be waived

Occasionally it is decided that a participant should be identified. Clive Wearing has suffered extreme memory loss following an illness. His real name is used when his case is cited, and this is a deliberate decision by his family. There may be other such cases. Sometimes people who take part in a study later identify themselves. This happened in the Zimbardo 'prisoner and guard' study.

Debriefing

At the end of a study, the participants should be debriefed. They should be told the aim of the study, what the procedure was, what results were obtained and how the results will be used. Then the participants should be asked again if they are happy to have their results included.

Right to withdraw

Participants must not be made to continue with a study when they would like to leave. They must be able to withdraw their consent at any time, and they must be told this clearly.

The right to withdraw is hard to apply in practice. Given what Milgram found about obedience, and what Asch (1956) found about conformity, it seems that once participants have committed themselves to take part in a study, they are reluctant to withdraw. They may know that they can withdraw in principle, but in practice there are social pressures that 'make' them continue. For this reason, they should be reminded periodically of their right to withdraw during the study.

Other guidelines

Other guidelines are equally important. For example, researchers should never work outside their level of competence and should not claim to know more than they do. They should check their ideas and intentions with colleagues to see what others think.

They should not cause distress to participants, and should make sure at the end of the study that all participants leave the situation not feeling worse than when they started.

Ethical guidelines: using animals

There are two ways in which animals can be studied: in their natural environment or in unnatural conditions. More ethical problems arise when animals are studied in unnatural conditions, although there are also guidelines for the use of animals in their own environment.

Studying animals in their own environment

Ethology is the study of animals in their natural setting. As long as they are not disturbed by being observed, this seems a relatively ethical way of studying them. In practice, ethologists do sometimes alter the environment to see what happens. For example, behaviourist John Watson carried out an experiment by moving a bird's nest to see if the bird would find it again. However, such experiments do not involve the same sort of manipulation that laboratory experiments do. For example, the nest was moved back and no lasting harm seemed to be done. Guidelines focus on issues such as not disturbing the animals and not affecting their normal habits. Special care should be taken regarding endangered species. Even straightforward observation can affect animal behaviour if the animal can sense that it is being watched. Some studies involve attaching transmitters to animals and this may affect the animal's behaviour. Therefore it should not be assumed that simply observing animals in their natural setting has no ethical problems.

Studying animals in a laboratory

Most ethical issues regarding the use of animals concern laboratory experiments. One argument is that animals should not be treated differently from humans. Another argument is that, given that animals feel pain just as we do, then we have no right to inflict pain on them. There are non-ethical arguments too, such as the point that animals are not exactly like humans, so it could be said that we don't learn much from animal studies in any case.

One ethical argument for using animals is that we should practise 'speciesism'. It is argued that we ought to put the interests of our own species before those of others and can therefore use animals in studies in which we would not use humans. There are practical reasons for using animals too: some species are easier to handle; some have a shorter reproduction cycle, so studying characteristics passed down through generations is possible. Some animals, such as rats, have all the same parts of the brain as humans do, so there is an argument that findings from such animals can be usefully applied to humans.

Guidelines are issued on the assumption that animals will be used in experiments. The guidelines concern issues such as caging and the care of animals, rather than whether animals should be used at all. Caging must be suitable for the species, and endangered species must not be used. In some circumstances, a Home Office licence must be obtained. There must be someone able to administer anaesthetics, and workers must be suitably qualified. Animal studies must take place only if no suitable alternative way of studying the issue can be found. No unnecessary harm must come to the animals and they should not experience any unnecessary pain.

General methods

You need to be able to describe what is involved in experiments, observations, questionnaires, interviews, case studies and content analysis. You should know advantages and disadvantages of each. It is a good idea to prepare two advantages or strengths and two disadvantages or weaknesses, as questions usually focus on one or two of these. Unit 6 is likely to ask for more information on these areas, so you will need this information then too. Usually candidates take Units 5 and 6 at the end of the course, and you will have already studied quite a lot about methods at AS, so you should be able to answer a wide range of questions on this 'general' area.

Table 1 gives a brief summary of possible methods and two advantages and two disadvantages for each. Remember that to score marks you need to express yourself clearly so, although the information here is only outlined briefly, when you are answering an examination question say clearly what your point is and give examples.

Table 1 An outline of methods, with examples of strengths and weaknesses

Method	Outline	Two advantages	Two disadvantages
Laboratory experiment	• Gathers quantitative data and follows scientific methods • IV is manipulated • DV is measured • Variables are controlled, e.g. participant and extraneous variables • Situation is highly controlled	• Reliable because controls mean it can be replicated • Cause and effect can be claimed (usually)	• Controls mean it is unnatural, so often not valid • Limited to IV and DV, so other factors are not examined
Field experiment	• As laboratory experiment, but the study takes place in the participant's natural environment or 'in the field'	• Natural surroundings • Still has controls	• Still unnatural • Participants may guess the purpose
Naturalistic experiment	• As laboratory experiment, but the IV is naturally occurring and not manipulated • Can be in natural surroundings	• Natural IV • Can be in natural surroundings	• Other factors are not looked at • Poor controls

Method	Outline	Two advantages	Two disadvantages
Observation	• Naturalistic, in that it is in the participant's natural surroundings (usually) • Overt (the one being watched knows about it) or covert (it is not known about) • Participant observation (the observer takes part in what is occurring) or non-participant observation (the observer stays apart) • Qualitative or quantitative data	• In a natural situation with real occurrences, so it is valid • Inter-observer reliability can be useful	• Participating observer can affect the situation • Difficult to observe everything and not to miss something
Questionnaire	• Set questions produced and everyone is asked the same • Quantitative data in the form of closed questions • Qualitative data in the form of open questions • Easy analysis for the most part and can reach a lot of people	• Everyone answers the same questions, so data can be compared • Can get qualitative data, so it is flexible	• The participant may guess what is wanted • May get the answers people think they should give
Content analysis	• Involves analysis of fixed content, e.g. newspaper article • Themes are looked for, e.g. by noting what is there and categorising	• Data are fixed, so findings can be checked • Usually ethical	• Limited application • Analysis can be subjective
Interview	• Can be set questions and a structured interview • Can be unstructured with only general aims • There is an interviewer to ask the questions • Usually gathers qualitative data in the form of a story, and responses can be taped	• Tends to get real data and not forced replies, so it is valid • Can help reliability if structured	• Can be hard to compare data from different people • Cooperation might mean that data are not valid
Case study	• Often uses many methods, e.g. interview, questionnaire • In-depth study looking at many aspects and following up issues and ideas • Often of one person or, if not, of one group • Qualitative data, given that a whole picture is required • Does not attempt controls, as requires in-depth thorough investigation	• Natural situation means that valid data are likely • In-depth data, unlike many other methods	• Hard to generalise to any other situation • Cannot claim a cause-and-effect relationship as many factors studied

Research methodology

You will already have learnt about many aspects of research methods and you need to check your understanding of the terms in the specification for Unit 3. You need to know at least one advantage and one disadvantage of the methods outlined below.

Participant design

There are three types of participant design: repeated measures, independent groups and matched pairs. These are ways of organising participants in a study.

Repeated measures design

The same participants do all the conditions. For example, participants learn both a random list of words and a categorised list and then their recall is compared.

+ The same people do all conditions, so the data can be compared without participant differences (e.g. they have the same memory).
– Order effects can occur. The practice effect means that the second condition is done best; the fatigue effect means the first condition is done best.

Independent groups design

Different participants do each condition. For example, some people have a random list and others have a categorised list and then their recall is compared.

+ No order effects occur. Each person does only one condition, so does not get tired or practised.
– Participant variables are not controlled (e.g. there may be memory differences between participants).

Matched pairs design

Different participants do each condition, as in an independent groups design, but pairs are matched in important ways — for example, by age, gender or education level.

+ No order effects occur. Each person does only one condition, so does not get tired or practised.
– People cannot be matched on all variables, so even if they are very similar there are still differences and participant variables may affect the results.

Correlational design

This is a different type of design where one score for a person is tested against another score for the same person — for example, reaction time against age.

+ Good for exploring variables that occur together naturally and can show up a relationship that can be further investigated.
– Shows a relationship but cannot show that one of the variables causes the other to change, i.e. cannot show cause and effect.

Sampling techniques

Usually, a sample is chosen from the target population. How that sample is chosen is important, as this may affect the findings.

+ A manageable study can take place, representative of the population.
– There is always the possibility that a biased group is chosen, so findings are dubious.

Random sampling

Everyone in the target population has an equal chance of being chosen.

+ Everyone in the chosen population has a chance of being in the sample. This is the best way of getting a fair representation.
– Not everyone is in the sample, so there is still a chance that it will be biased (e.g. regarding age, the number of people in the target population and the number chosen for the sample).

Systematic sampling

Choosing every fourth person on a register or every sixth person to walk past is an example of systematic sampling.

+ This is a manageable way of sampling. For example, if you choose every fifth person to come along (when doing a survey), this is a practical solution and reasonably fair as you will not be biased by personal preferences.
– This often involves people in one situation at a particular time, e.g. walking down the High Street on a Saturday morning, and this can cause bias.

Opportunity sampling

This is taking advantage of anyone available and is likely to be biased because many won't be there to be chosen.

+ It is manageable and quick, as you can choose whoever is available. This often means friends and acquaintances.
– Family and friends might be too cooperative and this might give bias to the findings as the participants are more likely to say what they think is wanted.

Quota sampling

To ensure a cross-section of the target population is picked, specific types are chosen, for example young females, young males, older males and so on.

+ The required types of people are selected and there will be a spread of different types (using the desired criteria), whereas other types of sampling may not ensure this.
– Choosing certain criteria and then finding people that fit those criteria does not necessarily mean that the people selected are representative of those criteria — they may have individual differences that give bias.

Volunteer sampling

People from within the target population are asked to volunteer for the study.

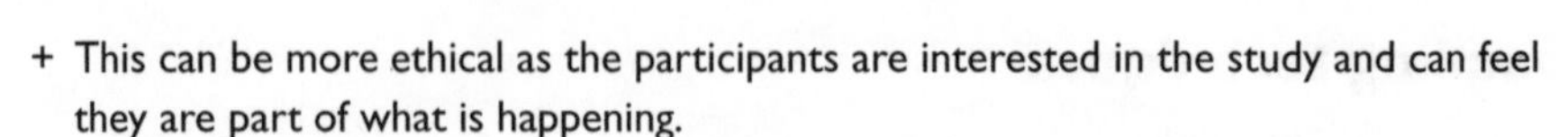

+ This can be more ethical as the participants are interested in the study and can feel they are part of what is happening.
– Volunteers are likely to be particular types of people, if only because they have time to take part in the study. They are not likely to be representative of the whole population.

Other terms

The other terms from the Unit 3 specification that you need to know regarding research methodology are described below.

Hypotheses (null, alternate, experimental)

The null hypothesis states that the independent variable has no effect on the dependent variable. It accounts for the results by attributing them to chance. For example, 'there is no difference in the number of words recalled whether they are presented in categories or randomly, and any small difference that is found is due to chance or some other factor'. The null hypothesis is tested using inferential statistics (see pp. 21–25).

The alternate hypothesis is a prediction of what will happen in a given situation. It is the alternative to the null hypothesis. If we can reject the null hypothesis as a consequence of obtaining a significant result from an inferential test, then we can accept the alternate hypothesis. For example, if we expect more words to be recalled when they are presented in categories, then the alternate hypothesis would be: 'there is a difference in the number of words recalled depending on whether they are presented in categories or randomly, and more words are recalled if the words are presented in categories'.

The experimental hypothesis is the same as the alternate hypothesis. It is called the alternate hypothesis when doing a survey by questionnaire, for example, but an experimental hypothesis when doing an experiment.

Independent variable (IV)

The independent variable is an aspect of the experiment that is manipulated by the experimenter. The independent variable in our example is the way the words are presented: as a categorised list or randomly.

Dependent variable (DV)

The dependent variable is what is measured by the experimenter, to assess the effect of the independent variable. For example, the words are presented in a categorised form or randomly (the IV) and the number of words recalled each time is measured (the DV).

Operationalisation of the IV and the DV

Operationalisation means defining the variables in terms of the operations taken to measure them. For example, it is difficult to measure helpfulness, but you could measure whether someone tells you the time or not. It is hard to measure whether people use organisation in memory, but you could measure whether they recall more words from a categorised list than from a random list of words.

Validity

Validity is the extent to which what is being measured and operationalised reflects reality. For example, if having a categorised list to recall really measures organisation in memory, and if telling someone the time really measures helpfulness, then the data will be valid. It is important to consider that an unnatural situation is unlikely to give valid data because the participants might be affected by the unnatural surroundings and not respond as they would in reality. If the situation is unnatural, you might say that the study lacks ecological validity. However, note that when measuring, for example, salivation in dogs, as Pavlov did, even though the situation was not natural, salivation was measured, so there is some validity in the study. Just because it is a laboratory experiment does not automatically mean that the study lacks validity.

As well as ecological validity there is face validity, which means that on the face of it the results seem to represent reality — they are what we would expect. Predictive validity means that the results do predict what will happen — again reflecting reality.

Reliability

Reliability can be tested by carrying out a study and then doing it again (test–retest). If the same results are obtained both times, then the study can be said to be reliable. With a questionnaire, half the results for each participant can be compared with the other half to see if both halves yield the same result (split-half reliability). Observer reliability may be achieved by having more than one observer using the same criteria. If the data from each observer give the same results, there is inter-observer reliability.

Generalisability

Generalisability is the extent to which findings from a research study can be applied to the population from which the sample was drawn, or to the population in general. If the sampling is correct, then the results should be generalisable. However, sampling is often not that good (see pp. 17–18). There are other issues too. For example, the target population itself is limited — perhaps being people in one situation or one culture, at one moment in time. So results might not be generalisable to other cultures at different times in different situations. Some studies use animals, so findings might not be generalisable to humans at all, although this should not be assumed to be the case, as there are many aspects about animals that we can generalise to humans.

Counterbalancing

Counterbalancing is an experimental procedure used to overcome order effects. Different conditions are presented in a different order. This is important in repeated measures designs. For example, if all participants learn a categorised list and then recall it, and then learn a randomised list and then recall it, they may always recall more words from the categorised list. This might not be because organisation aids recall but because they are tired by the time the second list is studied and recalled — this is the fatigue effect. On the other hand, the participants might all recall the words from the randomised list (the second list) better. This might be because they have learnt what to do by the time they do the second list, not because organisation does not aid recall — this is the practice effect. The fatigue and practice effects are called order effects because the order in which the conditions are presented affects the results.

Counterbalancing ensures that order effects will not be responsible for the results. For example, if one participant does the random list before the categorised list, and the other participant does the categorised list before the random list, then although fatigue and practice effects might occur, they would be evenly balanced. Therefore, if there is a difference in the recall, it is likely to be due to the IV (whether the list is categorised or not). Instead of counterbalancing, the order of presenting the materials can be randomised — chosen by tossing a coin, for example, which would have the same result. Counterbalancing avoids bias.

Situational variables and how to control them

A situational variable is a feature within the research setting that might affect the results of a study. If the study is a case study, situational variables might be part of what is looked at, so would not be controlled but would form part of the data. However, for many methods used in psychological research, such variables need to be controlled. When a cause-and-effect relationship is sought between an IV and a DV, situational variables must not be allowed to affect the results. For example, in an independent groups design in which one group is in a noisy room learning a randomised list and another group is in a quiet situation learning the categorised list, the amount of noise could affect the results. Situational variables include noise, temperature, lighting, time of day and the surroundings in general. For example, participants might perform differently in their natural environment compared with unnatural conditions.

Participant variables and how to control them

Participant variables, like situational variables, have to be considered and controlled. Participant variables are characteristics of individual participants that might affect results. They include age, gender, ability, lifestyle and job. For example, if a group of participants learning a categorised list have had more practice at remembering lists or have better recall than a group learning a randomised list, then the categorised list might be recalled better because those participants had better memories. Random sampling should control for participant variables, as should quota sampling to an extent.

Levels of measurement

Variables can be measured at different levels of detail. A **nominal** level of measurement is putting something into a category. An **ordinal** level of measurement is putting data into order or ranking them. An **interval/ratio** level of measurement is a real measure, where the data are measured using units of equal intervals — for example time, where seconds, minutes and hours are evenly measured.

For example, temperature can be measured in any of these ways. If we categorise room temperature as hot or cold, this is a nominal level of measurement. If we rate room temperature on a scale of 1 for very cold to 5 for very hot, then this is an ordinal level of measurement. If we use a thermometer to measure room temperature in degrees Celsius, this is an interval/ratio scale of measurement. You need to be able to say what level of measurement is used in a study.

Descriptive statistics

Descriptive statistics are used to represent data and can involve graphs/charts, calculating averages or displaying ranges. In the exam you might be asked to interpret such data, but it is unlikely that you will have to produce a graph.

Averages are measures of central tendency — they show how the data cluster around a centre point. You need to know about the mode, the median and the mean. The mode is the most frequent score. The median is the middle score. The mean is found when all the scores are totalled and then divided by the number of scores. You also need to know about the range of a set of scores — calculated as the top score minus the bottom score plus one. Table 2 gives an example for each of these calculations.

Table 2 Calculating the mean, median, mode and range

Measure of central tendency/range	Set of scores	Calculation
Mode	2, 2, **4, 4, 4**, 5, 6, 7, 8, 8, 9, 10, 10	There are three 4s, so the mode is 4
Median	2, 2, 4, 4, 4, 5, **6**, 7, 8, 8, 9, 10, 10	Middle score (median) is 6
Mean	2, 2, 4, 4, 4, 5, 6, 7, 8, 8, 9, 10, 10	Scores added together total 79; divide 79 by 13 (the number of scores) to give mean = 6.08
Range	2, 2, 4, 4, 4, 5, 6, 7, 8, 8, 9, 10, 10	Top score 10 minus bottom score 2 = 8; range = 8 + 1 = 9

Inferential statistics and related issues

Inferential statistics analyse the data and draw firm conclusions. Unit 5 looks at eight inferential tests. You do not need to know how to do the calculations but you do need to know which test to choose in a given situation and what the results of the calculations mean. Table 3 shows which test to choose. Note that simplified terms are used for each test (e.g. 'Wilcoxon', not 'Wilcoxon signed ranks matched pairs test').

Table 3 Choosing a statistical test

	Nominal data	Ordinal data	Interval/ratio data
Non-correlational designs			
Repeated measures design or matched pairs design	Sign	Wilcoxon	Related *t*
Independent groups design	Chi-squared	Mann–Whitney	Unrelated
Correlational design	N/A	Spearman	Pearson

Before you can use either of the *t* tests or the Pearson test, you need to know about normal distribution and standard deviation.

Normal distribution

A normal distribution indicates that the data are spread equally either side of the mean. In order to be spread evenly, the mean, median and mode must be similar. Normally distributed data show a bell-shaped curve (see Figure 1). The three tests for interval/ratio data (related *t*, unrelated *t* and Pearson) require more mathematical calculations than the other five tests, so the data must be normally distributed before these tests can be used.

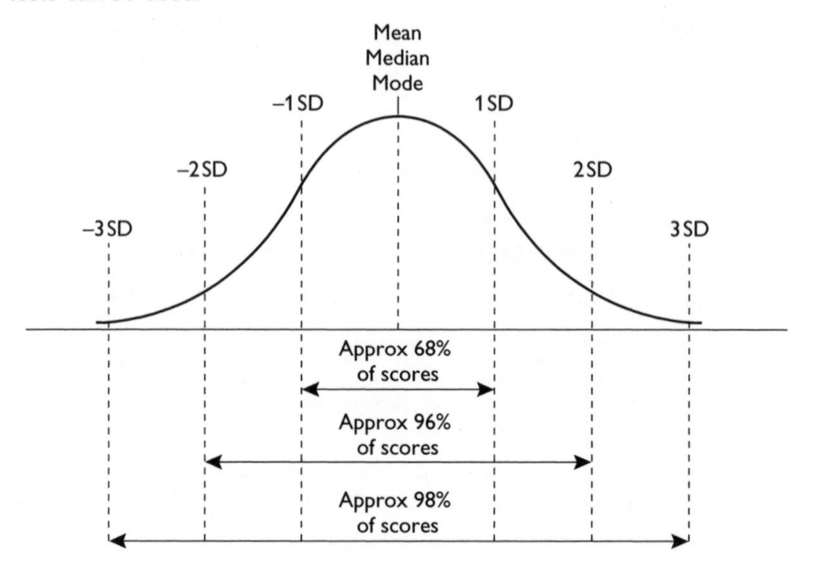

Figure 1 A normal distribution curve

Standard deviation

Standard deviation is linked to normal distribution. It refers to the spread of the scores around the mean, median and mode. The spread should be equal but we also need to know how the scores are spread, i.e. whether the curve is flat or steep. If the curve is flat and wide, the scores are spread widely; if the curve is tall and narrow, the scores are not spread far from the centre. When two sets of scores are compared using one of the three tests for interval/ratio data, *the spread of the two sets of scores must be similar*, again because of the mathematical calculations involved.

To calculate the standard deviation for a set of scores, first work out how much each score differs from the mean. Square the difference in each case and calculate the total of all the squares. Then subtract 1 from the number of scores. Finally, divide the total of the squares by the number of scores minus 1 to give the variance. The standard deviation is the square root of the variance.

The standard deviation shows how flat or steep the curve is, i.e. how far the scores vary from the mean. This tells us quite a lot about the data. To understand this, look again at Figure 1. The following argument assumes a normally distributed set of scores. You will see that around 68% of scores are within 1 standard deviation of the mean and 96% of scores are within 2 standard deviations of the mean. If we know what the standard deviation is, we can see where a score falls on that curve. For example, a child might score 60 on a test, but it is hard to know whether this is a good score or not. However, if we know that 50 is the mean and the standard deviation is 10, then we know that a score of 60 is in the top 16%, leaving 16% of scores better. If, though, the standard deviation is 2, then 60 is a very high score (most scores were clustered around 50), and if the standard deviation is 20, then a score of 60 is not that good (just above average). The standard deviation helps to put a score in context with the rest of the scores.

Table 4 shows an example of calculating standard deviation.

Table 4 Calculating standard deviation

Scores	Difference from mean	Square of difference from mean	Calculation
3	–3	9	(1) N = number of scores $N = 10$ (2) $N - 1 = 9$ (3) Total of squares of difference = 40 divided by $N - 1$ (9) = 4.44 (4) Standard deviation = square root of 4.44 = 2.11
4	–2	4	
4	–2	4	
5	–1	1	
6	0	0	
6	0	0	
7	+1	1	
7	+1	1	
8	+2	4	
10	+4	16	
Mean = 60/10 = 6		**Total = 40**	

Reasons for choosing inferential tests

The reasons for choosing a particular test have been outlined above. For example, you need to decide whether the study is a correlation or not. You need to know the design used, the level of measurement and, if the level of measurement is interval/ratio, you need to consider whether the data are normally distributed and whether two sets of scores have similar variance (both conditions must apply). Then, using Table 3, you can decide which test is appropriate. Tests apply to quantitative, not qualitative, data, so you would need to know that quantitative data were gathered.

How to rank data

Once you have chosen the right test, you can follow step-by-step instructions on how to do the calculations. For some tests you have to rank the data; for others you

have to square numbers and then square-root the total. The eight tests you need to know about use different calculations, but you will not have to do these in the examination. It might, however, be useful to know how to rank data; this is outlined in Table 5.

Table 5 Ranking scores

Scores	Rank of scores	Calculations
3	1	(1) Put the scores in order
4	2.5	(2) Rank them in order, giving the lowest score 1
4	2.5	(3) If there are equal scores (as for 4, 6 and 7), allocate the relevant rank equally between those scores. For example, the ranks 2 and 3 go against the scores of 4, so each gets 2.5
5	4	
6	5.5	
6	5.5	
7	7.5	
7	7.5	
8	9	
10	10	

Levels of significance

Once you have the result from a test, you need to find out whether the result is significant. To do this you need to choose a suitable level of significance. The level of significance is the percentage of results that you would accept as being due to chance and still accept that the study worked. If you are willing to accept that 5% of your results are due to chance but 95% of them are due to manipulating the IV, then your level of significance is 5%. If you are willing to accept only 1% as being due to chance, and you want 99% to be due to your manipulation of the IV, then your level of significance is 1%.

More precisely, the level of significance (if you accept 5% as being due to chance) is equal to or less than 5%, as you would also accept a percentage lower than 5% as due to chance. The way of saying that the level of significance chosen is equal to or less than 5% being due to chance is to say that the probability of the results being due to chance (p) is equal to or less than ($\leq$) 5% (0.05). This is expressed as: $p \leq 0.05$. If you chose 1%, this would be: $p \leq 0.01$.

One- or two-tailed

One more thing you need to know before being able to calculate whether the result of a statistical test is significant is whether the alternate hypothesis predicts a direction. If a direction is predicted (for example, if the hypothesis says that more words are recalled when a list is categorised), then this is a directional (one-tailed) hypothesis. If no direction is predicted (for example, if the hypothesis says that there is a difference in recall depending on whether the words are categorised or not), then this is a non-directional (two-tailed) hypothesis. This is important when deciding whether a test has shown significance or not.

Degrees of freedom

Some tests require you to determine the degrees of freedom before you can decide whether the result is significant. Calculations for degrees of freedom vary according to the test. For example, degrees of freedom for a chi-squared test are determined by taking the number of columns minus 1 ($c - 1$) and multiplying by the number of rows minus 1 ($r - 1$). In an exam you should be told how to work out degrees of freedom, or you may simply be told how many degrees of freedom are in the example given.

Critical value and observed value

The observed value refers to the result of the test calculations. For example, a *t* test gives the statistic '*t*' and an observed value might be $t = 1.889$.

To find out whether the observed value is significant, it must be compared with the critical value. You might have to do this in the examination. Critical values are given in tables. To find the right critical value you need to know whether to look along the 'one- or two-tailed' column, and you need to choose a level of significance. You also need to know either the number of scores in the set (*N*) or the degrees of freedom. In an exam, you should be helped with regard to whether the observed value has to be greater than or less than the critical value to be significant, as the tests vary. In a *t* test the observed value must be equal to or greater than the critical value.

To continue with the example where $t = 1.889$ and assuming that the hypothesis is directional (one-tailed), there are 9 degrees of freedom and the level of significance is 0.05 (5%), then the critical value with these conditions is 1.833, so the result is just significant. This means that the null hypothesis, which stated that the results would be due to chance, is rejected and the alternate hypothesis, which stated that the IV would cause any change in the DV, is accepted. The observed value (1.889) is greater than the critical value (1.833). These are the sorts of arguments that you must be prepared to give to say whether a given result is significant or not. Expect to be given a lot of the information, just as I have given the information in the example above, but without the explanation.

What 'it is significant' means

The *t* test requires the observed value to be equal to or greater than the critical value. If it is, then the result is significant. When we say the test worked and the result is significant, we mean that the null hypothesis is rejected and the alternate hypothesis is accepted. If the observed value is not significant (compared with the critical value), then the results are due to chance at that level of significance, or at least not due to what was predicted. So you state that the study did not work, what you said would happen did not happen and the results that were found could well be due to chance — the null hypothesis is not rejected.

Analysis of qualitative data

Qualitative and quantitative data

Quantitative data are analysed using descriptive and inferential statistics. Qualitative data also have to be analysed; they involve quality comments rather than detail about quantity. For example, counting the number of words recalled depending on whether a list was presented in categories or in a random form would involve quantitative data. Asking participants how they felt when learning both a categorised list and a randomised list (say, whether they found one list easier than the other and why) would be an example of qualitative data.

Subjectivity and objectivity

Objectivity refers to avoiding bias and not allowing personal opinions to affect the information gathered. Subjectivity is when personal opinions or judgements do affect the data. Objectivity is usually the aim. Scientific experiments aim to control all variables apart from the independent variable, and part of that control would be making sure that nobody's opinion or viewpoint affected what was found — so being objective is a control. It is unusual for subjectivity to be required, because if the researcher's perceptions affect the data then it could be those perceptions that led to the findings.

Analysing qualitative data

Qualitative data involve descriptions and comments — the sort of information that can be presented in the form of a story. However, when there is a large quantity of data (as there frequently is when qualitative data are gathered) then presenting all the information is not likely to be a practical approach. A summary using analysis is more useful. It is helpful to find themes within the story, so that there are specific areas of focus.

Interviews, observations and case studies yield qualitative data. A researcher gathering qualitative data will take steps to record accurately what is said or done, to avoid subjectivity, and analysis has to assume that the data have been collected carefully. However, it is unlikely that all the data will have been recorded by the researcher, so already there may be an element of subjectivity.

Triangulation

One useful point about qualitative data is that more than one method is often used to gather information. Usually there is also a longitudinal approach. An interview might be backed up by an observation or by an analysis of documents. The term for arriving at the same findings using more than one means is *triangulation*. Triangulation improves both reliability and validity.

Collaborative research

Another way of checking data is for the participant(s) and the researcher to work together. The data are recorded and the researcher writes up the story in collaboration with the participant. In this way the researcher can be sure that the data are clear and accurate from the participant's point of view. The data are likely to be valid, if the participant agrees, and they are likely to be reliable because another researcher working with the same participant should achieve the same results.

Grounded theory

Even with the use of triangulation and collaborative research to improve reliability and validity of data, there is a need to develop themes, as outlined above. This is the task of the researcher. One way to remain true to the data gathered is not to start with a specific hypothesis. Instead of having a clear statement of what is expected (a hypothesis), the researcher has only a general aim. For example, the general aim might be to investigate how a certain team structure works. Data are gathered by a researcher attending meetings, by interviews with team members, perhaps by analysing previous minutes and so on. Once the data are gathered, the researcher looks for themes. A theory can emerge, grounded in the data.

In order to derive a theory or themes from such data, all statements and comments must be analysed. This is done by identifying the main points of all comments and sorting data into these main points or themes. At this stage there can be subjectivity, and the researcher should keep notes about how themes were developed. For example, if a childcare setting is being studied, one theme might include attachments, where comments are made about how well the child gets on with the play leader, or if the child responds better when its mother is present. Another theme might be communication, where comments are made about parents not knowing how to respond, or how children interact with one another. Some statements may not be easy to categorise and might be noted down under a general 'other' category. If this process is undertaken carefully, analysis into themes can be highly successful. Following analysis, themes might be linked to theory (such as attachment theory), and thus it can be seen that in this way theory comes from such data.

Application A: Child psychology

Attachment

Babies appear to form close attachments. Attachment is a two-way process: the baby must form a bond with the caregiver and the caregiver must also bond with the baby. There is some debate about whether babies form a single attachment with the main caregiver or whether they make multiple attachments.

Evolutionary basis of attachment

Imprinting in precocial animals

Lorenz (1935) found that geese imprint on the first moving object they see, usually their mother. Imprinting is the term used for the 'following' instinct. In evolutionary terms, imprinting is a useful survival instinct for all precocial animals (precocial refers to any species where the newborn can move about and the sense organs are well developed at birth). As the newborn animal follows its mother, it will be taken care of. Those with the imprinting instinct are more likely to survive and to reproduce, so the instinct is likely to be passed on in the genes.

Evidence that newborn babies quickly identify their mothers

It is thought that attachment is a form of imprinting and can be explained in evolutionary terms. Human infants who attach to their mothers, and who in this way 'persuade' their mothers to attach to them, have a better chance of survival, so attachment could be said to be a survival instinct. Klaus and Kennel (1976) found that newborn babies who had extra skin-to-skin contact with their mother within hours of birth appeared to develop stronger attachments. This suggests a biological basis for attachment.

Stranger fear and separation anxiety

If attachment is a process that aids survival of the newborn infant, the infant should bond with its mother and recognise her almost immediately, and there is evidence for this being the case. There should then be a mechanism to strengthen the attachment at the stage when the infant becomes mobile and might move away, and so might become vulnerable to predators. It has been found that babies from around 6 months old (the time they start to become mobile) develop both a fear of strangers (stranger fear) and anxiety when separated from their main caregiver (separation anxiety). These mechanisms discourage the baby from being far from its attachment figure.

Evaluation

+ Studies have shown that newborn babies can recognise their mothers at an early stage and that skin-to-skin contact leads to stronger attachment. This is evidence that attachment is an instinct.
– Attachment may be formed through social pressure, as mothers are expected to bond with, and attach to, their babies. It may not have an evolutionary basis. There is a nature/nurture issue here.
– Human infants seem to form more than one attachment. This goes against the evolutionary explanation, which suggests that the natural mother is likely to be the attachment figure.
+ However, the ability to form multiple attachments might be additional evidence for there being an evolutionary basis for attachment, as having more than one attachment figure might improve survival.

Bowlby's theory of attachment

Bowlby's ideas follow a psychodynamic approach in that a child's early years are considered to be critical, especially the early mother–child relationship. Bowlby observed that when babies and young children were separated from their mothers they experienced strong emotions related to loss. These emotions seemed to start with great distress; if the separation continued, this distress turned to despair. If the child remained apart from its main caregiver, this despair turned to 'disattachment' or detachment. Bowlby drew these conclusions from observations of, for example, children in hospitals (at the time of his studies, parents were not encouraged to stay in hospital when their children were ill) and from undertaking clinical interviews with young adolescents asking about such separations.

Bowlby thought that attachment was an evolutionary process. He observed how young apes clung to their mothers, and even when they were a bit older their mothers were used as a base from which to explore. Bowlby thought that this was the type of behaviour that human babies would display if they were not separated from their mothers.

Monotropy and stranger fear

Bowlby concluded that a single caregiver would form a unique attachment with the child and that this forming of an attachment is an instinct. The notion of a single caregiver is called **monotropy**. Bowlby thought that stranger fear and the idea of an infant clinging to a safe base from which to explore are survival traits. Clinging to the attachment figure also helps in the attachment process — hence the idea of attachment being a two-way process.

Critical period

Bowlby thought that there is a critical period to form an attachment and if this critical period is missed, then no attachment will form. This idea reflects what ethologists studying animals in their natural setting had observed — that some behaviours such as imprinting seem to have a critical period and once this period has passed, such behaviour does not occur. According to Bowlby, mothering is needed before the child is 12 months old; once the child reaches the age of around 2 years, it is too late. This idea of a critical period has been criticised by others.

Evidence for Bowlby's maternal deprivation hypothesis

Bowlby drew his conclusions from various studies, two of which are outlined below.

Goldfarb (1943) compared children who were fostered immediately after leaving their mothers with children who were fostered at the age of $3\frac{1}{2}$ years, having been in care. The children were matched on areas such as mother's level of education and occupation. Those fostered later were behind on many measures such as language use and social maturity, as well as IQ. This was said to show that children in institutions, where they had been looked after in groups, did less well than children who had the chance to form attachments before the age of 2.

Harlow and Harlow (1969) studied young rhesus monkeys. One well-known study involved four young monkeys who received milk from a 'mother' made of wire and four who received milk from a 'mother' made of wire covered with terry towelling. All the monkeys had enough food but all preferred to hold onto the terry towelling 'mother'. This study is said to reinforce the idea that infants want comfort and attach to a mother-figure for reasons other than the need for food.

Evaluation

+ Both the above studies suggest that very young children need attachment to a safe figure, and they need comfort as well as food.
+ Other studies (such as Spitz, 1945) have drawn the same conclusions.
– The Harlows' study was carried out on monkeys. Therefore, it could be said that the findings cannot be applied to humans.
– The Goldfarb study looked at children who were fostered quickly compared with those who were not. Perhaps there was something about the early fostered children that led to them being chosen, and perhaps that something affected their later development too (e.g. they might have been more attractive).
– Children in institutions were usually under-stimulated and it might have been the lack of stimulation that led to the slower language development of the late-fostered children in the Goldfarb study, rather than maternal deprivation.

Attachment types, including cross-cultural issues

Bowlby suggested four stages of attachment. The first phase is pre-attachment, up to around 6 weeks after birth; the attachment in the making phase is from around 6 weeks to 6 months; this is followed by the clear-cut attachment phase, up to around 18 months; and finally the phase of reciprocal relationships, from about 2 years onwards. Stranger fear is a characteristic of the second phase (attachment in the making); separation anxiety is a characteristic of the third stage (clear-cut attachment).

It has been suggested that there are different attachment types — attachment can happen in different ways, some more successful than others. Mary Ainsworth looked at attachment types in different cultures by means of cross-cultural studies. There are problems with this type of research, including understanding between different cultures and finding methods that suit more than one culture.

Strange situation test

Ainsworth developed the strange situation test to investigate different attachment types. She looked at children of around 12 months old and how they interacted with their mother or the main caregiver. The idea is that the child plays with its mother and then a stranger is involved in the interaction in various ways. The important thing is how the child reacts to the stranger and to the mother. A typical test involves the child playing with its mother, when a stranger enters the room. The stranger talks to the mother and interacts with the child. The mother then leaves the room and the stranger distracts the child. The mother returns and the stranger leaves. Then the mother leaves so that the child is alone, the stranger comes back in and then the mother returns. This gives a lot of different variations, and hidden observers watch how the child reacts in the various situations. These reactions are used to identify different attachment types.

Types of attachment

Securely attached children are happy when their mother is present, and even with the stranger there, but get upset when the mother leaves the room. The stranger cannot comfort the child. When the mother returns, the child goes straight to her and needs comfort. It is thought that about 65% of American middle-class children show this attachment type.

Anxious-avoidant attachment is characterised by the child not checking that the mother is still there when just the mother and child are together and the child is playing. Children with an anxious-avoidant type attachment do not cry when the mother leaves the room and strangers can comfort the child. The child may turn away from the mother when she comes back into the room. Ainsworth et al. (1978) suggest that about 23% of middle-class children in the USA have this attachment type.

The third type of attachment identified by Ainsworth is **anxious-resistant**. These children seem anxious even with the mother present. They are upset when the mother leaves but do not get comfort from her return. They go to her for comfort but pull away. 12% of the American children studied by Ainsworth et al. (1978) showed this type of attachment.

Evaluation

– These studies can be criticised on ethical grounds as the children become very upset. However, the mother soon returns and it could be said that this situation is similar to reality.

– The sample in the Ainsworth et al. (1978) study consisted of American middle-class families. Care should be taken when generalising the findings to other types of family, or to different cultures. Cross-cultural studies suggest that there are problems transferring this method to different cultures — see below.

± The three attachment types identified by Ainsworth are organised types. However, it is thought that attachment is not always organised. Current research looks at disorganised attachment. A disorganised type occurs where children are maltreated and where there is no predictable parenting.

Attachment types and caring style

Cross-cultural studies and parenting style

Cross-cultural studies can help to show whether a characteristic such as attachment applies to all human development (has a genetic cause) or whether a characteristic develops through environmental and cultural influences.

Tip

You can use the evidence from cross-cultural studies to discuss the nature/nurture argument, which is one of the issues you need to debate for Unit 6.

The strange situation test has been used to see whether the attachment types found in the USA by Ainsworth are also found in different cultures. In 1967, Ainsworth used the strange situation test with Ugandan mothers and children, and also looked at attachment types in Baltimore, USA. She found three attachment types in both cultures: securely attached (secure), insecurely attached (resistant) and not yet attached (avoidant). Ainsworth noticed that the avoidant children had mothers who were with their children less and who gave less physical contact. She concluded from her observations that mothers who were most responsive had babies who 'talked' more (used more gestures and so on) and cried less. Different parenting style seemed to affect the type of attachment.

Sagi et al. (1985) used the strange situation test to study children who lived in kibbutzim. These children are looked after collectively during the day by a nurse/carer, rather than having their mothers with them most of the time. Sagi et al. found that around half the children were anxious-resistant and only around a third were securely attached. These figures contrast with those of Ainsworth et al., and it was concluded that this different parenting style affected the type of attachment.

Evaluation

+ Using the same procedure (the strange situation test) in different cultures can produce different results, in this case different patterns of attachment between cultures. Since the method is the same, it is concluded that parenting style causes the different attachment patterns. Cross-cultural studies are useful in differentiating the characteristics we are born with from those affected by different cultural habits.
- It could be claimed that the method itself gives rise to the results. Perhaps the strange situation test gives particular results in one culture and is understood or reacted to differently in another culture.
- The strange situation test can be upsetting for participants, especially perhaps in particular cultures, depending on the normal interaction between the mother, the child and strangers. This raises ethical issues.

Parenting styles

Cross-cultural studies show differences in patterns of attachment types. Although the attachment types themselves are similar, the way in which they are distributed varies. If we accept that a secure attachment is best, then it can be claimed that some parenting styles are better than others. For example, Ainsworth's findings suggest that responsive parenting is best. 'Responsive' means using appropriate physical contact and being around most of the time. Ainsworth and Bell (1969) looked at mothers' behaviour and found that some mothers were more responsive than others. Responsive mothering (at around 3 months, for example) seemed to produce more securely attached children at 12 months. Responsive mothering was characterised by being sensitive to the baby's feeding needs, being responsive to the baby's signals, and giving positive emotional signals and appropriate responses.

Evaluation

± Attachment is a two-way process and it could be claimed that a mother may be more or less responsive depending on the child's temperament.

The father's role

The child is likely to form attachments with others too, not just with the mother or main carer. Research suggests that the father, for example, has a different role and that there is a different process of attachment. Lamb et al. (1987) suggested that in families where the father spends around a quarter of the time with the child that the mother does, the father is not less sensitive to the child's needs. Fathers are likely to spend more time playing with the child, rather than having the same caring role as the mother. Cox et al. (1992) found that fathers are just as likely to be securely attached to the child, if they are sensitive to the child's needs. The father might have a different parenting style, or different role, but can still have a strong attachment to the child.

Deprivation and privation

Defining privation and deprivation

Privation refers to the situation where a child has never had an attachment figure. This can happen if the child is raised in an institution from birth or in cases where parenting is so poor as to be deemed non-existent. It is not that the child is *deprived* of care and attention — none was received in the first place.

Short-term deprivation refers to a situation where there is an attachment figure but the infant is deprived of that person's attention for a short time. Bowlby studied children in hospital. At the time of his research, parents did not stay with their children in hospital. He also studied children when their mothers went into hospital, perhaps to have another baby. Again, at that time, children did not visit as they do now. Short-term deprivation is really separation and the attachment figure returns.

Long-term deprivation is when the separation continues for some time. If a separation continues for months rather than weeks, then it is considered to be long term. It is hard to distinguish long-term deprivation from privation as it is rare for an infant to be privated. In other words, there is usually at least some form of care.

Short-term deprivation

Infants who are deprived of their main attachment figure for a short time tend to follow a pattern of responses. First, the child cries and becomes distressed. Next comes despair: although the infant is calmer, it is clear that he or she is very upset. The final stage is disattachment or detachment: the child appears to get over the separation and turns to others for comfort. It may seem as though the child has

recovered from the separation, but in practice Bowlby thought that detachment led to problems. When the attachment figure returns, the attachment may need to be formed again from the beginning. If short-term deprivation is not too long, this stage may not be reached.

Evaluation

± **Bowlby's approach was a psychodynamic one. If you have studied mood disorders for clinical psychology, recall the psychodynamic explanation concerning loss, as this applies here. If not, then consider the psychodynamic approach: how early experiences are important, and how early problems in moving through the stages can lead to fixation at certain stages and to later problems if defence mechanisms act to repress memories and difficulties.**

The effect of short-term deprivation depends on the age of the infant at the time of separation. The greatest effect is from around 6 months to 3 years. Consider the importance of stranger fear and separation anxiety. Gender also has an effect — boys appear to become more distressed than girls.

The more stable the relationship, the better the child can cope with short-term deprivation. Children who have experienced separation before cope better. If the child is with others with whom he or she has formed attachments, such as members of the extended family, then the effects of short-term deprivation are reduced. The effects are also less severe if the attachment figure introduces the child to those who will take over the care and prepares the situation beforehand.

Evaluation

– **Studies looking at short-term deprivation take many factors into account and are not controlled. Observation and interview are generally used. There can be subjectivity in judging the amount of distress shown by a child. Few children are studied, and it is hard to draw conclusions because of this.**

Effects of day care

Day care can be seen as short-term deprivation. The consequences of day care depend on whether the situation is prepared by the main attachment figure and on the age and gender of the child. The temperament of the child is a factor too. Children can gain confidence from day care as well as suffer from short-term deprivation.

Kagan et al. (1980) concluded that day care in itself does not cause a problem, if there is an adequate number of staff and if the children are stimulated. Well-equipped and well-staffed provision seems to help children develop in an intellectual sense.

In addition, mothers who prefer to work are happier, and this can be a good thing for the child. It is also thought that children who attend day care are more sociable, more independent and more able to cooperate with their peers. However, poor-quality day care can affect a child adversely.

Evaluation

- It is hard to generalise to all day care settings given the differences between them. Individual staff members can easily affect the whole experience for the child.
- Follow-up studies are rare, and conclusions are drawn from a particular study at one time. Although short-term deprivation is being studied, the long-term consequences are also of interest, and follow-up studies are needed.
- When considering the effect on intellectual development, it should be noted that IQ cannot be measured before the age of around 2 years. The developmental quotient (DQ) is measured instead. It is hard to judge intellectual progress, and difficult to separate the effects of day care from other influences.
- Children who attend higher-quality day care often have parents who are more involved in their care than children who attend lower-quality provision.

Long-term deprivation

Studies of long-term deprivation look mainly at the effects of parental separation and divorce and parental death. Young children who experience long-term deprivation show separation anxiety and move through the stages of distress, despair and detachment. Unlike short-term deprivation, where the stage of detachment might either never be reached or might be overcome if an attachment is reformed, in long-term deprivation the stage of detachment is likely to be reached.

The death of a parent may have less severe consequences than parental separation or divorce because there is less likely to have been stress between family members before the event. Divorce might affect a child more because the child feels anger, whereas when a parent dies, there is a different family reaction and the child may be old enough to understand that the parent did not leave intentionally. Other family members are more likely to offer help and support when a parent dies, but with divorce a large part of the family is sometimes lost to the child.

Hetherington et al. (1979) suggested that there is a crisis phase with regard to divorce, when fathers tend to indulge the child and mothers become more demanding, less affectionate and more aggressive. According to Hetherington, this phase is followed by the adjustment phase, which occurs around 2 years later: the mother becomes calmer and more patient; an arrangement might be made with the father; and the situation is more equable. The conflict between the parents in the crisis phase seems to be the problem rather than the separation itself. It is likely that fathers who remain with children go through the same phases.

Bifulco et al. (1992) looked at women who had lost their mothers before they were 17 years old, either through death or separation. These women were more likely to be depressed than those who had not lost their mothers. It seems, therefore, that such a loss has an effect later in life. This agrees with the psychodynamic explanation of how loss can lead to depression.

Family reordering

A possible problem with parental death, divorce or separation is that the remaining parent finds another partner and family reordering can occur. It has been suggested that the real cause of problems are family disputes rather than the actual divorce or separation. Cockett and Tripp (1994) carried out a study using a control group of children who lived with their natural parents, some having a home life with no conflict and others having a home life with arguments. Then they looked at children in reordered families, where the parents had divorced and remarried and there were step-brothers and step-sisters. The children from reordered families were found to have more health troubles and problems at school. They also showed lower self-esteem than the control group. It was not that the control group children had no problems, but the children in reordered families had more. Children living with their natural parents and little conflict did best, so it was concluded that the disagreements that come before and during divorce are what cause difficulties.

Evaluation

+ The Cockett and Tripp (1994) study used a control group that was matched for age, gender and socioeconomic status, so the sampling was done carefully. It also looked at children with natural parents who did not have conflict in the home and some who did — which was a further control. This was, therefore, a well-designed study.
- Although children in the reordered families had experienced divorce, they also had to reform into a new family with step-brothers and step-sisters, and this may have been the problem rather than the divorce or the conflict.
- There was a correlation between divorce/reordering and health and school problems. However, correlations do not show a cause-and-effect relationship, so we cannot say that divorce causes health and school problems.
- Reordered families can have money problems and other difficulties, so stress as a result of these factors, rather than divorce, could be the cause of problems.

Other reasons for problems include a parent not adjusting well or a child having poor resources for coping. How children react to divorce and reordering of families might depend on the relationship they have with their parent(s), and some parents are better at communicating about a break-up than others. Hetherington (1993) found that the child's age, gender and parents' emotional state all affected how well children responded to their parents' divorce.

Effects of privation

Studies of privation usually involve children who were brought up in institutions. Privation means there has never been an attachment. Children who are adopted after a certain age but previously lived in an institution have also been privated.

Some studies suggest that the effects of privation are not reversible and once a child is affected by the lack of an attachment figure, then their later character will be affected. Other studies suggest that the effects are reversible.

Table 6 Studies looking at the effects of privation

	Study	Outline
Privation is not reversible	Goldfarb (1943)	Children fostered early were compared with children fostered later. The institutionalised group did not have an attachment figure and were privated. At age $3\frac{1}{2}$ years, the institutionalised group were behind in measures of IQ. They were still behind at ages 10 and 14.
	Spitz (1945)	Children in South American orphanages had no attachment figure and little stimulation. They were apathetic and lethargic. Children with no attachment figure in hospitals were also developmentally delayed.
	Harlow and Harlow (1969)	Four rhesus monkey infants could get milk from a wire 'mother' and four could get milk from a cloth 'mother'. All of them preferred to cling to the cloth mother and it was thought that the infants needed comfort as well as food.
	Bowlby (1946)	44 juvenile delinquents who were also thieves were compared with a group of delinquents who had not committed a crime. 14 of the 44 who had committed a crime appeared to have an affectionless character. Nine of these had been maternally deprived when young. It was thought that maternal deprivation caused this affectionless character.
Privation is reversible	Skeels and Dye (1939)	25 children in an institution who had been privated from birth were studied. 13 of them, when they were 2 years old, were sent to another institution where retarded women lived. These 13 were looked after by the women. They gained in IQ compared with the group who stayed in the institution. In fact, when they were older they had gained even more, and they did better as adults.
	Tizard and Hodges (1978)	Children from an institution who at the age of 2 were either adopted or went back to their natural families were followed. Most formed some attachments but the adopted children were more likely to do so, perhaps showing that good quality care helps.
	Koluchova (1972)	Twin boys entered an institution at a very young age. At about 18 months they went back to live with their father and a stepmother. They were badly treated and locked away. Found at age 6 years, they did not speak and were malnourished. Back in an institution they caught up a bit, but did really well when fostered by two sisters. They were given good quality care and their IQ improved to above average, showing that the effects of early privation can be overcome.

	Study	Outline
Privation might be reversible to an extent	Curtiss (1977)	Genie was badly treated and locked away. She was found at age 13. She was looked after by psychologists, who tried to encourage her to use language. They succeeded to some extent but by no means completely, and she did not catch up or become 'normal' although she was given good quality care. This suggests that the effects of privation can be overcome to an extent but not completely — or perhaps by the age of 13 it is too late. Maybe there were problems that would have occurred in any case.

Social development

Play and categories of play

Very young babies cannot be said to play but there is sometimes infant-to-infant interaction at around 6 months old, depending on the culture and whether, for example, there is an extended family nearby. Hartup (1983) found that around 25% of infants have not interacted with another infant by 6 months, and around 20% have contact once a week. There is a pattern to how babies react to one another. At around 3 months old they seem to react to the cries of another baby and at around 6 months old they smile at other babies. They are only really sociable with one another when there are toys present and when they begin to play. Table 7 outlines different types of play.

Table 7 Types of play

Type/category of play	Brief description
Solitary/individual play	Playing alone and focusing on muscle activity or learning activities; solitary play decreases as the child gets older
Onlooker play	Watching others rather than participating; onlooker play decreases with age
Parallel play	Playing alongside other children but not being involved in a game with them; may involve imitating another child; parallel play decreases with age
Associative play	Playing with and sharing with other children; associative play increases as the child gets older
Cooperative play	Playing structured games with other children; the games have specific rules; cooperative play increases with age
Reality play	The most common form of play in 2 year olds — play without fantasy
Fantasy play	Fantasy play is more likely than reality play in 3 year olds

Type/category of play	Brief description
Social fantasy play	Fantasy play merges with social play; children get together and agree themes
Mastery play	According to cognitive-developmental theory, children in the sensorimotor stage engage in mastery play, where they learn to coordinate their muscle movement appropriately
Symbolic play	According to cognitive-developmental theory, children in the preoperational stage engage in symbolic play and pretend games
Play with rules	According to cognitive-developmental theory, children in the concrete operational stage play with rules and the rules are not flexible

Factors affecting children's play

It can be seen from Table 7 that age affects the type of play a child engages in. Other factors that affect play include gender, environment and parental encouragement. Young children tend to play with others of their own gender. The environment affects children's play. For example, with large toys that encourage muscle movement, social groups are larger and play is noisier (Vandenberg, 1991) compared with toys that encourage quieter play. Parental encouragement can also affect the type of play. A study by Sutton-Smith (1981) of the history of families who settled in a new country (New Zealand) showed that, at first, the children were left to themselves and drew up their own games. Later, when the adults had more time, they became involved in structuring the children's play.

Nowadays, television and commercial toys tend to structure children's play. When a parent joins in pretend play, the child is likely to play for longer and try out roles with more confidence.

Theoretical perspectives on play

The cognitive-developmental approach

Tip

Recall your AS material on the cognitive-developmental approach and in particular the material on Piaget. Recall the four main stages and consider what types of play might suit children in the different stages.

According to Piaget, the type of play a child engages in depends on the stage of development of that child. Table 7 outlines the three main types of play according to the cognitive-developmental approach (mastery play, symbolic play and play with rules) and links them to the appropriate stage. Play is part of developing both cognitive and motor skills. In a new situation, play can help a child to learn (to assimilate and accommodate). According to Piaget, there are four stages of cognitive development. These are the sensorimotor stage, the preoperational stage, the concrete operational stage and the stage of formal operational reasoning.

Evaluation

± To evaluate the cognitive-developmental approach to play, you can use the same evaluation points that you would use for the approach per se. The theory of play rests on the idea of Piaget's stages, and any criticisms of that idea would be criticisms of the theory of play.

The psychodynamic approach

Tip

Recall your AS material on the psychodynamic approach and in particular the material on Freud. Recall the basic assumptions about the importance of the unconscious and the defence mechanisms that help to repress unconscious thoughts. Recall also the psychosexual stages, and concepts such as the Oedipus complex and the id, ego and superego.

According to Freud and the psychodynamic approach, any problems are likely to be caused by conflicts that have been repressed and are hidden (and inaccessible) in the unconscious. These conflicts are likely to have come about through some sort of fixation at one of the psychosexual stages. The psychodynamic theory of play is that children act out their unconscious thoughts through play — the child resolves conflicts between the id and ego by acting them out. This area is researched by Melanie Klein and Anna Freud. Play can be cathartic, in that anxieties can be released. It can also allow defence mechanisms to work: for example, feelings can be projected onto dolls, and emotions can be worked through.

The therapeutic value of play

One way of relieving problems is to make unconscious thoughts conscious by uncovering them. The problem is how to uncover unconscious thoughts: methods include dream analysis and free association. The individual has to help in the analysis and accept what is revealed during psychoanalysis. However, young children are unlikely to have the ability to accept analysis. One method used to uncover unconscious thoughts in children is play therapy. Children's unconscious thoughts can be accessed by observing their play, and analysis can take place by interpreting their play using psychodynamic concepts.

Axline (1971) carried out a case study on a child she called Dibs. The child was very disturbed and Axline watched his play carefully. The child played with toys that could represent the family, such as dolls. Axline looked for evidence of family conflict. Such conflict seemed to be shown, for example, when Dibs buried a doll face down in a sandpit. The doll seemed to represent Dibs's father. Hostility seemed to be released through play, and through using such examples Axline was able to uncover conflicts and problems.

Evaluation

± To evaluate the psychodynamic approach to play, the same criticisms can be used that would be used to evaluate the psychodynamic approach per se. For example, the concepts of id, ego and superego are not measurable, so are not subject to scientific testing, which can be seen as a criticism. Similarly, analysis involves subjective interpretation, for example, when Axline interprets the burial of the doll as being symbolic and referring to Dibs's relationship with his father.

Friendships

Friendships seem to start after the age of 2 years, and this links to the stages of play. As children engage in associative and cooperative play, by definition, they play more with friends. These types of play are likely to start between the ages of 2 and 3. Hartup (1992) describes friendship as involving affection, reciprocity and commitment, and people must see themselves as equals. Friendships help children to gain information about themselves and others, they help in developing social skills, they provide models for later relationships, and they enable a child to have fun. Friends seem to have common interests, they communicate clearly with each other, they exchange information and they can resolve conflicts.

Developmental trends

Friendships change as children develop. It is useful to use Piaget's stages to consider this. In the sensorimotor stage, children are unlikely to have friends, although they do interact with other children, as outlined earlier. From the age of around 2, they may begin to develop friendships. Young children expect their friends to like what they like, as would be expected from an egocentric child in the preoperational stage. By the concrete operational stage (from around the age of 6) children are likely to know that others may not feel the same as they do. They can allow for differences between themselves and their friends. Between the ages of 7 and 9, friendships tend to be between children of the same gender and age. Young children tend to have a best friend but older children develop multiple friendships. Up to the age of around 5, children are likely to form friendships because they want to share a toy, or for other similar reasons, whereas older children form friendships because they like someone.

There are gender differences in friendships too. Girls share more intimate details than boys. Friendships tend to form between children who live near one another (proximity) and those who are similar to one another (similarity). Friendships tend to be between children of the same age, gender, culture and interests.

Cultural differences in peer relationships

There are cultural differences in peer relationships. For example, being shy in British culture might lead to a child being rejected or neglected, whereas in China shy children are not rejected (Chen et al., 1992). Children prefer to be with others who are similar to themselves, and this includes those of similar culture. One cultural difference involves whether a society is collectivist or individualist. In Israel, for example, a kibbutz is a collectivist subculture, but other subcultures in Israel, such as the middle class, focus on the individual. In a study by Shapira and Madsen (1969), children from these two different subcultures were encouraged to play together in groups of four.

The game meant that the children had to cooperate to succeed. There were six trials for each group. The first three trials were set so that prizes were given at the end only if the group succeeded, and then they were all rewarded. The second three trials involved prizes for individual effort during the game. In this second set of trials, individuals gained more reward if they worked for themselves than if they worked for the group, although the group needed to cooperate to achieve the overall goal in all six trials. The kibbutzim children set up cooperative rules and stuck to them in all six trials, to achieve the overall aim. Those from the individualist subculture preferred to focus on getting prizes for themselves. It was concluded that socialisation patterns affect friendship patterns because they are likely to affect how a group will behave, especially with regard to rules in games.

Popularity of individual children

The popular child

Some children are good communicators and interact with others straightaway. These children have good social skills, including making others laugh, and tend to be well-liked. Such children tend to be good at schoolwork too. There seems to be a link between having a good relationship with parents and forming positive relationships with others. Physical attractiveness is also a factor — attractive children are often more popular. Even names can have an influence, and children with fashionable names are likely to be popular.

Evaluation

± The self-fulfilling prophecy predicts that children become more physically attractive if they are popular.

± Confident children are likely to become popular, and popular children are likely to be confident too.

Rejected and neglected children

In contrast, the rejected child is often rejected straightaway for inappropriate behaviour and tends to remain rejected. Other children are simply neglected — it is not that they behave inappropriately; they are just not accepted. Neglected children tend to be shy and are not good at social interactions with other children. They do not try to join a group, whereas popular children watch for a while and then join the group, using appropriate behaviour. Rejected children do try to join a group but tend to behave aggressively and are rejected, as aggression is usually inappropriate.

Evaluation

± Different groups value different behaviour. Even aggressive behaviour can be valued by some groups, so it is not easy to judge what makes a child popular or rejected; it depends on the group norms. A rejected child does not conform to the norms. It is not so much aggressive behaviour that leads to rejection as inappropriate behaviour.

Application B: Environmental psychology

Personal space and territoriality

Personal space is the area around an individual where, if another person enters that space, it makes the individual uncomfortable. The size of the area defined as personal space depends on various factors, such as how well two people know one another. The better you know someone, the closer they can come to you without making you feel uncomfortable. Alpha personal space is the measured distance and beta personal space is the subjective estimate of the distance. The area around us into which we do not want people to come is called our body buffer zone.

Territory is defined by personal space and by other boundaries such as actual fences or areas that we consider belong to us. We can define our territory even in public places. For example, on a beach we might spread out towels or other belongings to delineate our territory, which we would then defend.

Hall (1966) listed eight categories of distance at which we would still feel comfortable if someone was near to us, given how close we are to them in other ways (see Table 8).

Table 8 Hall's categories of distance

Distance from the person	Category	Example
0–15cm	Intimate distance — near phase	Intimate contact
15–45cm	Intimate distance — far phase	On very close terms
45–75cm	Personal distance — near phase	On good terms
75–120cm	Personal distance — far phase	Social interactions between friends
1.2–2m	Social distance — near phase	Meeting a friend's friend
2–3.5m	Social distance — far phase	Business transactions; not wanting to be friends
3.5–7m	Public distance — near phase	Lecturer with audience
Over 7m	Public distance — far phase	Meeting someone with higher authority

We don't actually work out the distance at which we feel comfortable with others but we feel uncomfortable if certain people come within a particular distance of us.

To measure personal space, we can be asked at what distance we would feel comfortable if someone approached, or we can be asked to place 'figures' at certain distances.

These simulations and experiments are the sorts of studies carried out to investigate this area. Naturalistic observations are also carried out and it is sometimes possible to measure actual distances in these real situations.

Evaluation

+ Naturalistic observations are more valid as there is a natural setting.
+ Simulations and experiments mean that many variables can be controlled, so the study is likely to be replicable and it might be possible then to show reliability.
- Simulations and experiments lack validity, as the situation is unrealistic. The measure is more about feelings than distance, so it is difficult to represent in an unnatural situation.
- Actual measurements are difficult to carry out and it may be hard to determine the exact relationship between the two people.
- If observations take place in a crowded setting, the impact of the crowd might affect personal space (e.g. if there is no room to maintain a comfortable distance).

Cultural differences in personal space

It could be that personal space is instinctive — keeping our distance from those we know less well might be a good survival trait. However, as distances involved in personal space seem to vary between cultures, it is likely that personal space is learnt through culture and customs. Hall thought that every culture had this idea of personal space and that people of all cultures are more comfortable when those they do not know well keep their distance. This could be evidence for the concept of personal space being innate. However, Hall also suggested that the actual distances involved are learnt through cultural expectations.

Watson and Graves (1966) looked at two Arab students and two American students. The Arabs maintained a shorter distance than the Americans and touched each other more. Some cultures are called contact cultures because individuals touch more during interactions and have a smaller body buffer zone. American culture is a non-contact culture, whereas Spain, Morocco and Latin America are contact cultures (Watson, 1970).

Evaluation

- It is difficult to know what is meant by culture (e.g. a Latin American culture is mentioned but there are cultural differences between Latin American countries).
- It might be religion or some other difference that confers variations in personal space, rather than culture.

Individual differences in personal space

There are gender differences in personal space. Girls seem to develop boundaries more quickly than boys. Men appear to have larger body buffer zones than women. It is possible that men are more upset than women when their personal space is invaded. Age also affects personal space, with older children requiring a larger area.

People who suffer from schizophrenia or other mental illness seem to have more variation in their personal space areas, but findings differ. For example, one study found that those with schizophrenia had a larger body buffer zone, whereas another study found that the personal space of someone with schizophrenia was either larger or smaller than that of an individual without a mental illness, rather than always being larger. Another study suggested that a greater degree of schizophrenia seemed to mean a larger body buffer zone.

Aggressive people tend to have larger body buffer zones. This means that more people are likely to invade their space and this might even account for the aggression.

Consequences of invasion of personal space

'Fight or flight' response

Individuals respond to invasion of their personal space in different ways; this might involve an instinctive reaction to do with the 'fight or flight' response connected with arousal and survival. For example, if someone sits close to another person, the other person is likely to move away quite quickly, as if following a 'flight' response (Sommer, 1969). Those reacting with aggression might be showing a 'fight' response. The flight response is more commonly found.

Helping behaviour

According to Konecni et al. (1975), people are more likely to pick something up for someone else if their personal space is not invaded. On the other hand, Baron and Bell (1976) found more helpful behaviour if someone's space was invaded, so these two findings are contradictory.

It has already been shown that there are different personal distances depending on the relationship between people, so this could be a factor — how does the helping person view the person in need of help?

Importance of territory

By controlling the space around us we can protect our privacy and maintain a concept of self in relation to others. According to Altman (1975), territorial behaviour can help to avoid conflict too. Three types of territory are outlined in Table 9.

Table 9 Three types of territory

Type of territory	Type of control	Example
Primary	Frequent use, long-term occupancy; used for important and personal activities; claim to ownership	Own bedroom, private office or own flat
Secondary	Regular use for some time	A church or park near home
Public	Temporary use for a limited period; not much claim to ownership	Bench when waiting for a bus or a seat on a bus

In animal research, the term used is territoriality — this refers to actual space that is defended. Territory, however, does not have to refer to actual space. For example, it could refer to ideas that we want to defend by using copyright laws.

Using territory to obtain privacy

As suggested above, one function of territory is to protect privacy (Altman, 1975). Privacy allows us time to view ourselves in relation to others, and to build a concept of self. There are different types of privacy: desired privacy is what we choose, in the sense of how far we are willing to interact with others; achieved privacy is the privacy we actually get. If our achieved privacy does not match our desired privacy, then we are not satisfied. In some cases we desire interaction with others, and so we are less protective; in other cases we do not desire social interaction and we erect barriers (physical or other) to protect our privacy. For example, a pile of books in the library can act as a barrier. Body language can also be used to protect privacy and territory; for example, by turning away, or placing elbows on a desk.

Using territory to ease social interactions and to avoid conflict

A related function of territory is that it acts as a social organiser. We can build our concept of self by obtaining privacy and distancing ourselves from others. We can also make sure that we are part of a culture by fitting in with rules of privacy and territory.

This links with the idea of defending territory according to the costs and benefits of doing so. With animals, when the costs of defending a territory are high, resources are generally shared. For example, if the territory is large and resources are scarce, then a lot of energy would be needed to defend it. However, if the area is small and resources are plentiful, it might be worth defending. Interactions in humans are more complex. It might seem, for example, that even when resources are plentiful we share them. However, social conventions are sometimes used to define who can share the resources, and in fact the resources are being defended, even if not by physical means. An example of this is where Bushmen invite others to share what they have but have rituals for gaining access, and this in practice limits those who can share the resources.

One way of protecting resources and of easing social interactions is to avoid conflict. Protecting territory can be a way of avoiding conflict. The street gang theory suggests that territory is held by different gangs or groups. Conflict can occur between bordering territories and territory can then change hands. In this way, gangs or related groups are likely to take over larger territories and conflict is less likely to occur as ownership is between fewer (or related) gangs. Thus territory becomes a social organiser and conflict is avoided.

The effect of architecture on behaviour

Building design, the environment and residential satisfaction

Building design can affect behaviour and this is considered when looking at the idea of defensible space later in this section. The environment can also shape behaviour.

Both the environment and building design can lead to more or less residential satisfaction. For example, a detached home links with the concepts of privacy and territory: territory is clearer and privacy is more likely to be achieved. This might not be the case in some styles of housing, such as high-rise flats, where there are communal areas.

People generally prefer to live in socially homogeneous groups, with like-minded people. However, if groups of people live together and have the same difficulties or needs, then there can be heavy demands on particular services. For example, if all the families have young children, there is pressure on primary schools. There may also be more group conflicts if, for example, groups are segregated according to ethnic background. There may be an uneven demand on resources and in-group/out-group conflict between areas. Such conflicts can be avoided to an extent by each area having its own centre and its own structure. A grid design is based on this theory and helps to ensure that areas are similar in size and have equivalent facilities.

Defensible space

In terms of residential satisfaction, the idea of defensible space is an important concept. Newman (1991, 2003) says that defensible space means dividing public space into areas that people feel they own. Individuals and small groups come to see what was previously public space as their own personal or private space, or at least as secondary territory. This means that they are likely to defend these areas and crimes are less likely. It is also possible that people gain a new respect for the territory of others, as they then have a territory of their own to look after and which they want others to respect.

In high-rise buildings many of the areas are public. If these public spaces were 'owned' by residents, there might be less vandalism. Newman points out that the idea of defensible space is not about fencing but about reassigning areas so that residents take ownership of them.

Newman suggests that it is important to make sure that any common space is at least overlooked by residents, that symbolic markers are used to delineate territory (such as low walls), and that the appearance of housing and environments is such that residents can take pride in living there. Newman presents three case studies to show how these ideas about defensible space can lead to greater residential satisfaction and reduced crime. One case study involved Clason Point in the South Bronx, in New York City. A row of houses within a public housing project had an area in front of it that was maintained publicly. It had been turned into dirt ground and was used by drug gangs. Fencing, curbs, paths and lighting were introduced and the ground was reallocated for the use of individual residents. This led to a reduction in the overall crime rate of 54% in the first year after the changes. Another case study involved an area called Five Oaks in Dayton, Ohio. Streets were closed off by gates and this led to them being seen as part of the housing. They were then 'owned' and defended. Newman points out that it is important that the residents are involved too; it is not enough just to close streets off to traffic. The third case study concerned the Yonkers

area in New York. High-rise buildings were pulled down and families were rehoused in town houses in middle-class neighbourhoods. The new designs had to be integrated with existing housing and residents had to be encouraged to look after their grounds. In all three of these case studies, the idea of defensible space led to improved resident satisfaction, and in some cases crime rates were reduced too.

Evaluation

- Many variables are involved in measuring resident satisfaction and it is hard to conclude that defensible space principles cause any differences. Newman's findings have not always been replicated. Since these are field studies, variables cannot be controlled.
- It is assumed that residents will defend space if it is delineated, and that criminals avoid secondary or primary territory. These assumptions may be incorrect.

Bad practice in architectural design

One well-known example of poor architectural design is the Pruitt–Igoe housing project in St Louis, Missouri. The housing project consisted of 3000 apartments in 43 high-rise buildings. On the face of it, the project was well designed: there was enough room and the grounds were pleasant. However, the area quickly became run down and within 3 years only 30% of the apartments were occupied. Squatters had moved in and public areas such as stairwells were misused. Yancey (1971) studied the project. The residents seemed satisfied with the apartments: 78% said they liked them, compared with 55% who were satisfied with the slums in which they had lived previously. The problem seemed to be the overall design, which did not suit the way people lived. The areas where people could meet were situated away from the apartments, and this was not how people used to chat in their back yards in the slums. Friendship groups failed to develop. It was concluded that a good design should take account of the residents' behaviour. For example, a means for friendships to be formed needs to be provided. The principles of defensible space can be used to ensure that play areas and communal areas are seen as 'owned' territory and are used as such.

Evaluation

+ Another study emphasised the way in which planned communal play areas and planned semi-private space can lead to visiting between neighbours. Wilner et al. (1962) looked at a project in Baltimore that had apartments on 11 floors, as did the Pruitt–Igoe development, but there was more planned communal space, and more residential satisfaction.

Good practice in architectural design

An example of good planning is the Eastlake housing estate in England (Halpern, 1995). The Department of the Environment wanted to improve an area of houses and flats built in the 1960s. Before a plan was drawn up, a questionnaire was designed and interviews carried out to determine what improvements people living in the area wanted. The residents helped to decide the priorities.

To measure whether asking residents to contribute to decisions in this way meant better satisfaction, residents were asked how helpful they thought their neighbours would be in certain situations, such as if they were burgled or if they needed to talk to someone. It was concluded that such questions measured mental health, and it was thought that getting resident involvement in such projects did improve mental health (as measured by responses to such questions). The idea of residents being involved in decisions about improving their neighbourhood should mean that public areas are seen as being owned by the residents, and the principles of defensible space suggest that this will lead to a more pleasant environment in which to live.

Evaluation

- Many factors are involved in issues like building design. It is difficult to point to one factor, such as resident involvement in planning, and say that it has caused any improvement in mental health. Other factors, such as the characters of the residents themselves, could lead to the improved resident satisfaction.

Stress, crowding and urban living

It has already been suggested that high-rise living can lead to problems, especially if certain issues, such as enabling friendship groups to form, are not addressed. Principles of defensible space can be used to try to improve resident satisfaction. Halpern's study of the Eastlake housing project has suggested that giving residents power over decisions concerning their environment can improve mental health. However, crowding, as might occur in apartment blocks, and urban living itself can lead to stress, as can other environmental factors.

Sources of stress in the environment

Noise

It has been shown that even quiet noise can be stressful. Noise is defined as any sound that the listener does not want to hear. People can adapt to certain noise, such as sounds in the office and around the home. However, if they are not able to prepare for the noise or have not had time to adapt to it, then it can be stressful. Well-practised tasks are less affected by noise than more complex tasks.

Glass and Singer (1972) carried out an experimental study looking at the effects of noise on performance. Tasks involved verbal reasoning and mathematical skills. Different groups experienced different conditions while doing the same tasks. One group was subjected to loud noise, the other had soft noise. Sometimes the noise was random and unpredictable, sometimes it was regular. Some participants were able to control the noise by pressing a button. The participants had to solve puzzles; some puzzles had no solution — to make the participants frustrated. They also had to proof-

read some text. The participants who had the loud, unpredictable and uncontrollable noise did least well. This is called an environmental after-effect.

Evaluation

+ The findings show that uncontrollable and unpredictable loud noise affects our ability to do complex tasks. This agrees with common sense, and so would seem to be a natural finding, even though the study involved an unnatural task and manipulation of variables.
+ Field studies looking at children's cognitive abilities in natural situations where there is noise and in quieter areas reinforce the findings of Glass and Singer (1972). It seems that noise does affect cognitive functioning.
– This was an experiment and the tasks were imposed on the participants, so the situation lacked reality. This means the validity of the study could be criticised.

Maser et al. (1978) carried out a field study looking at the effects of noise on performance. In contrast to Glass and Singer's (1972) study, this involved a real situation, so the findings have more validity. Maser et al. compared school children near an airport and found that those with low aptitude achieved lower test scores compared with a control group in a quieter area. Another study showed that children in a classroom near a railway line did less well than other children. Both these findings suggest that noise affects learning, or at least performance.

Heat

People can become more aggressive in hot weather, although aggression levels tend to fall again in extreme heat. Harries and Stadler (1983) found that cases of aggravated assault in Dallas increased on warmer days. Another study in a natural situation considered how much time drivers spent honking their horns (a measure of aggression). The time spent honking horns behind a car stopped at a green light increased as the temperature rose. Bell and Fusco (1989) found that the number of assaults increased as the day became hotter, but after a certain (high) level of heat it fell. Laboratory studies have been carried out to investigate the effect of heat on behaviour. Page (1978) looked at helpfulness and found that less help was given in hot conditions. Cunningham (1979) carried out a field study looking at helpfulness and found that people were more willing to be interviewed at a pleasant temperature than when it was hot. This finding supports Page's laboratory study. Fisher et al. (1984) found that people were less willing to help on a cold day too, so it may be extremes of temperature that affect us. Note, however, that Fisher et al. were looking at helping behaviour and not at aggression, so we cannot conclude that there is more aggression at extremes of temperature. Studies suggest that heat, not cold, brings out aggression.

Evaluation

+ Findings of controlled laboratory studies support those of field studies where natural situations are looked at. This means that findings are likely to be valid.
– Crimes considered in the above studies (and in many studies) involve violence and aggression. It may be that not all crime increases as the temperature rises.

Effects of environmental stressors on behaviour

Mathews and Canon (1975) found that people were less helpful when there was a noisy mower nearby, even if someone needing help appeared to have a broken arm; so noise seems to affect helping behaviour. Appleyard and Lintell (1972) found that there was little social activity among residents in a street with heavy traffic noise and the residents said that living there was lonely; so noise seems to affect the level of social activity.

Strategies for coping with environmental stress

Removing the source of stress

Clearly, if noise is a stressor, one way of coping is to remove the noise, although this is often not possible. Practical solutions such as installing triple glazing may help. However, this is not a psychological strategy for coping with stress — if the source is removed, then the stress does not need to be coped with. It should be noted that removing the source of stress is preferable to having to cope with it.

Controlling the stressor

It is often not possible to remove the source of stress, and this can actually add to the problem. Brady (1958) studied pairs of monkeys to see whether having control over a situation reduces stress. The 'executive' monkey was able to turn off a machine that delivered electric shocks several times each minute; the 'passive' monkey could do nothing about the shocks. Brady found that the monkey with the power to turn off the electric shocks (which turned off the shocks for both monkeys) was more likely to develop ulcers than the monkey with no control over the situation. This finding is said to explain why decision-makers are prone to develop ulcers. However, the study was criticised because monkeys that had shown more switch-pressing behaviour before the study began were chosen as executive monkeys. This may have meant that the executive monkey's temperament was different from that of the passive monkey, so temperament rather than the situation may have caused the results.

Other studies replicating Brady's did not achieve the same results. Weiss (1971) carried out a similar study and found that 'executive' monkeys (those able to do something about the stressful situation) had fewer ulcers. The findings of the two studies are clearly contradictory, but it is apparent that control over a situation does affect how much stress is felt. As Weiss's study involved random allocation of monkeys to the executive and passive condition, and found less stress if there was control, it is tempting to suggest that controlling a situation is a way of coping with stress.

Problem-focused and emotion-focused coping mechanisms

Coping mechanisms tend to be seen as either practical or emotional. Practical coping mechanisms involve focusing on the problem, for example removing a stressor or gaining control over it, as outlined above. If an environment is too hot, individuals can move, or if there is too much noise at work, they can change their job. These

sorts of actions are problem-focused strategies for coping with stress, as they involve focusing on the problem itself. Emotion-focusing involves controlling one's emotional response to a situation. One defence mechanism mentioned below is suppression. This involves making a conscious effort not to think about the stressor. If a situation that is causing stress is necessary, suppression may be a good emotion-focused strategy for coping with that stress.

Defence mechanisms

From your AS studies of the psychodynamic approach, recall what defence mechanisms are. You should be able to say how they are ways of coping with stress.

Defence mechanisms include repression, rationalisation, displacement, denial and projection. It is not easy to deny when an environment is excessively hot or noisy but some people are able to intellectualise — that is, they can explain to themselves why they are accepting a particular source of stress. Intellectualisation is a defence mechanism that involves thinking about something at an intellectual and distant level, rather than at a more personal level. Suppression involves a conscious effort to avoid thinking about stressful things, and avoiding focusing on a stressor (such as noise) is likely to be a good way of coping.

Evaluation

± Problem-focused strategies are best when the situation can be changed. However, it is not always possible to change job or move house. If there are no practical solutions, emotion-focused strategies are best.

\+ Studies support the idea that having control over a situation or being able to predict it can reduce the experience of stress (e.g. Glass and Singer, 1972).

– Some studies are carried out using animals and care should be taken when generalising findings from animals to humans.

Tip

Many environmental psychology studies focus on stressful situations and their effects, such as crowding and the effects of high-density living that follow this section. Use the findings of these studies to draw conclusions about the stress from such situations for individuals, and draw conclusions about coping mechanisms.

The effect of crowding on animals

One well-known study of the effect of crowding on animals was carried out by Calhoun (1962). Calhoun set up a 'rat universe' consisting of four pens within a block 10 feet by 14 feet. Female rats divided themselves among the four divisions but a few dominant male rats controlled two of the pens. This left the rest of the males living in the other two pens, where rat density was subsequently greater. These two pens were called behavioural sinks, partly because the behaviour of the rats in them was so bad. As the rat population grew, disease and behavioural disturbances also increased, and there was a high infant mortality rate. Over-population was found in all pens but even more so in the behavioural sinks where packs of deviant males became homosexual, cannibalistic, hyperactive and hypersexual.

Other studies of the effect of crowding on animals have found self-destructive behaviour (Dubos, 1965) and decreased fertility (Snyder, 1966). It is generally found that an animal population will expand to a certain level within a particular size of environment and then stay at that number, usually because overcrowding leads to the death of some of the animals and/or greater infant mortality.

Evaluation

+ Different studies into the effect of crowding on animals have shown similar results — the animals' behaviour seems to be affected by crowding, and population growth is limited. When studies find similar results, they reinforce each other's findings.
+ This was an experiment with good controls, so cause-and-effect findings can be claimed.
– Findings from studies of animals may not be generalisable to humans. Calhoun (1971) suggests that animals are designed (genetically) to respond to crowding in a certain way, and humans may not have that same genetic make-up. Humans are affected by social and cognitive factors.
– It could be claimed that animal studies such as the one carried out by Calhoun (1962) are not ethical. Infant rats died and other rats became cannibalistic.

Effects of high-density living on humans

One form of crowding that has been extensively studied in humans is high-density living, which is also seen as stressful. Of course, people can be crowded and yet not stressed, especially if the crowding is by choice. If crowding is by choice, then this is usually short term.

Density is the term for the number of people in a defined space. Whether a person feels crowded does not necessarily depend on the density of people in the space. People with a large body buffer zone might feel crowded in a situation when other individuals do not. High-density living refers to there being a large number of people in a limited space. This usually means that people feel crowded.

Social density refers to the number of people in a space and **spatial density** refers to the size of the space. Higher spatial density means less space for the same number of people; higher social density means more people for the same space. So someone living alone in a small space would experience high-density living.

As has been suggested, animals react badly to high-density living. However, animals are less cognitive than humans, and their behaviour is more likely to be from their genetic/biological make-up than from thinking and planning. This means that humans might react to high-density living in a different way from animals.

High-density living and poor health

Studies of humans in high-density living situations have shown that there is physiological stress and arousal. Measurements of blood pressure, skin conductance and sweating can show such stress and arousal. High-density situations such as football matches lead to arousal, but it is not a bad thing when people seek out such situations, and it is usually only short term. So physiological arousal might not necessarily mean ill health for the individual. However, most studies do show a link between high-density living and poor health, as they are carried out in situations where high-density is likely to lead to stress and problems and tend to include long-term situations. If nothing else, living together in close proximity can mean disease spreads more quickly. Fuller et al. (1993) carried out a study in Thailand and found that feeling crowded was linked with ill health, even if the actual density was not that high. Individual differences are important here — some people need more personal space than others. So the emotion of feeling crowded is important, as is the actual density of the situation. Lepore et al. (1992) found that mental health was affected by crowding, especially when perceived control was low. This is an interesting finding that links to ways of coping with environmental stress, which were considered earlier in this section.

Evaluation

+ Many studies show a link between high-density living and poor health.
– Feelings of crowding are important, as well as actual density.
– Most studies look at high-density and negative situations. Few have looked at high-density and positive situations (e.g. pop concerts), so finding negative responses to high-density living is more likely.
– Many factors are involved when trying to find a cause-and-effect link between high-density living situations and ill health. There might be a correlation, but the cause might not be the density itself.

High-density living and alcohol use

Studies suggest that people living in groups drink more than people living alone (e.g. Donelly, 1978). In the USA, more people die of cirrhosis of the liver in higher population density living conditions (Foster, 1990).

Evaluation

– It is hard to point to high-density living itself as the cause of more alcohol use, as there are other possible causes such as stress or mental health problems. However, high-density living might be the cause of the stress.

High-density living and task performance

Studies have looked at performance of tasks according to the number of people present, i.e. according to the density of the situation (which is not exactly the same as high-density living). Evans (1979) studied people, in an experiment, working on tasks in conditions of either one person per square metre or six people per square metre; this was the measure of density (the independent variable). Performance of complex tasks was affected more than performance of simple tasks. In another study, participants were asked to learn to trace a maze while people watched (Knowles, 1983). Learning rate decreased as the size of the audience increased. However, a large audience may not be the same as a high-density situation. Although the rate of learning was lower with a larger audience, it was also found that these participants forgot less in the break time. Audience size was thought to represent social density. These studies suggest that people will do better at work if they are not subjected to a large audience, or when they have more space to work in.

Evaluation

– Experiments looking at when there are people nearby or not may be measuring something about the effect of an audience, which is not quite the same as the effect of long-term, high-density living, so the validity of such studies can be questioned.

The effect of high-density living on social behaviour

High-density living can increase aggression, especially in males and if it lasts for some time. In experiments where short-term, high-density situations were created, participants showed aggression, for example by giving a hypothetical criminal a longer sentence. One study considered whether people were more likely to violate someone's personal space when the social density (number of people) was increased. It found they were, though not in low spatial-density situations when the size of the space was large enough. Invading someone's space is taken as a measure of aggression, and it is concluded that there is more aggression if a situation has high social density. Cox et al. (1984) found a close relationship between high-density living in prisons and aggression in male prisoners.

Evaluation

+ More than one study has shown a relationship between high-density situations and aggressive behaviour, so the studies reinforce each other's findings, and are evidence for one another.
+ Field studies are more valid. For example, when looking at whether personal space is invaded, the study used the number of people around as a measure of social density, and that seems to be a valid measure.
– A problem with some of the experiments outlined above is that the high-density situation is created and not natural, so validity might be questioned.
– Not only are the situations in experiments unnatural, but what is looked at is short-term density, so they are not a very valid measure of high-density living.
– In some field experiments the measure of aggression was whether someone's personal space was invaded, and this might not be valid.

Crowd behaviour in humans

Crowding is when people get too close and an individual's personal space is invaded. Crowding suggests a negative emotion — something we do not like. When there are a lot of people in a small space but we are happy with the situation, then this is not

crowding. Theories of crowd behaviour involve not only crowding (a negative emotion) but also the positive emotions of having others close by.

Contagion theory

We lose our identity in a crowd. As part of a crowd, we revert to instinctive behaviour, and such behaviour is primitive and not civilised (LeBon, 1903). This idea links to Freud's views. When civilised, we are under the control of the superego. However, if we revert to instinctive behaviour, that control is not available. If crowd behaviour allows our instincts to control our behaviour, we are likely to be more aggressive and less controlled than usual. The leader of a crowd can replace the superego and might take control. Under these conditions, ideas spread rapidly between members of the crowd — they are contagious.

Deindividuation

The theory of deindividuation refers to the way that people in a crowd lose their identity as individuals. This links to LeBon's ideas outlined above, although it does not claim that ideas are contagious. According to Jung (1946), individuation is the development of individual personalities. Festinger et al. (1952) used the word deindividuation to mean when individuals do not express individual personalities. Zimbardo (1970) suggested that behaviour becomes impulsive and disinhibited when people in groups lose their identity.

Some studies support the idea that deindividuated people act in a different way. Festinger et al. (1952) found that participants were more negative about their parents when they were dressed in a grey labcoat in a poorly lit room than when the lighting was normal and they were wearing their own clothes. Diener et al. (1976) looked at the behaviour of children when 'trick or treating' at Halloween. When the children's names and addresses were known, they obeyed instructions, such as to take just one sweet (only 8% disobeyed). However, when the children were deindividuated, in that their names and addresses were not known, 80% disobeyed and took more than one sweet.

It is concluded that being deindividuated increases the likelihood of aggressive or antisocial behaviour. This can happen in crowds, so helps to explain why people in crowds do things they would not normally do.

Evaluation

+ This theory helps to explain why some individuals in crowds behave in an antisocial way that seems out of character. There has been evidence from well-controlled studies to suggest that deindividuation is a cause for antisocial crowd behaviour.
– Zimbardo (1970) found that soldiers who were deindividuated by wearing hoods and cloaks were less willing to harm a confederate of the experimenter than they were when wearing their usual uniforms. This may have been because they were deindividuated normally (in uniform), so when they were disguised they were less deindividuated. However, this does seem to be an unusual conclusion.

- Johnson and Downing (1979) found that nurses, deindividuated by not wearing a name badge, did not harm people more (by giving more shocks). In fact, they tended to give fewer shocks when deindividuated. This also goes against the claim that deindividuation leads to more antisocial behaviour.
- Experiments have used a hood and cloak to deindividuate participants (e.g. Zimbardo, 1970). This may have reminded participants of groups such as the Ku Klux Klan, so may have encouraged them to act accordingly (the Ku Klux Klan is associated with racist and antisocial behaviour).

Emergent norm theory

According to emergent norm theory, it is not that people in a crowd revert to instinctive (antisocial) behaviour, but that a norm emerges from the crowd, and crowd behaviour is, like all behaviour, governed by social norms (Turner, 1974). At first a crowd is just a collection of individuals, but as distinctive behaviour emerges, norms develop and then crowd members conform to those norms. As individuals within the crowd start to conform, others come under pressure to follow the majority. Distinctive behaviour, by definition, stands out and is likely to be aggressive or antisocial, but not necessarily so. This theory can explain why people in a crowd do things they would not normally do.

Evaluation

- Individuals in a crowd are usually deindividuated and yet to conform to emerging norms they would have to be self-aware (Diener, 1970).
- Crowds get together for a reason, so social norms are already involved (Riecher, 1982).

Changing behaviour to save the environment

Why behaviour is often not environmentally friendly

A current question in environmental psychology is 'Why do we often behave in a non-environmentally friendly manner?' If resources are used too freely, it may lead to a shortage, especially if the resource is not quickly renewable. One way of protecting resources is to ensure that they are not freely available.

It is usually much easier to use resources than to conserve them. Behaving in a non-environmentally friendly manner can either be 'taking', for example cutting down trees, or 'giving', for example dumping rubbish. This sort of self-serving behaviour is commonly found. Not only is it easier to be environmentally unfriendly, but it is also positively difficult sometimes to behave in an environmentally friendly way. For example, finding a litter bin or taking rubbish to an appropriate place can be time-consuming.

Reasons for behaviour being environmentally unfriendly include the following:

- Some resources are freely available and not owned by others or taxed by the government, such as forests in some areas of the world or fishing in certain waters. This means that behaving in an 'unfriendly' manner is easy and quick. This is called 'taking' or 'harvesting' resources. If such resources take a long time to renew (or are not renewable), clearly this is a future problem.
- Future problems are not always focused upon, in the way that short-term problems are. Environmental problems are often future problems — 'out of sight is out of mind'.
- 'Giving', such as dropping litter, is often quicker and easier than behaving in an environmentally friendly manner.
- Actively seeking out an environmentally friendly solution can cost time and/or money. For example, unwanted waste might have to be taken some distance to be disposed of, or there might be a charge for disposal (e.g. of scrap metal).
- There may be insufficient knowledge of environmental issues. Tindall and O'Connor (1987) found that a better understanding of the issues led to more cooperation in terms of environmentally friendly behaviour.
- When people are unsure of a situation, it seems that they are likely to act in their own self-interest (Fleishman, 1988). If they have an understanding of the issues and behave in an environmentally friendly way, then others are likely to conform to that good behaviour.

Ways of changing attitudes

Rewards and punishments

One way of changing attitudes is to introduce a reward system, and perhaps to set up a penalty system for non-cooperation. If environmentally friendly behaviour were a reward in itself, then most behaviour should be cooperative. However, as stated above, in the short-term, self-interest tends to be rewarded. It is quicker to drop litter than to find a bin, and it is easier to throw things out without sorting them. To change such behaviour, it is necessary to make sure that people are rewarded for it. People can be rewarded for acting in a cooperative manner or for not acting in a non-cooperative manner. Wit and Wilke (1990) found that punishments and rewards were equally effective, and perhaps a balance of both is needed. An example of a reward system is where those driving cars with more than one person in them are given special (quicker) routes, which means that drivers of cars without passengers are punished. An example of punishment is a fine for dropping litter, while a reward for not dropping litter is a tidier area in which to live.

Evaluation

– Studies tend to be simulations or small-scale pilot studies, so the results cannot always be generalised to every situation and all people.

Persuasive communication

Lack of knowledge about environmental issues can lead to non-cooperation (if we don't know something is bad, then we won't avoid it). Making sure that people know about environmental issues might be a good way of changing attitudes and encouraging more environmentally friendly behaviour. Gifford (1997) listed the advantages of good communication regarding environmental issues:

- It reduces distrust.
- Penalties for non-cooperation can be agreed.
- Group identity is enhanced.
- Rewards for cooperation can be set out clearly.
- It allows for agreement over who benefits from resources.

One model of how to change attitudes — the Yale approach — looks at persuasive communication. Developed by Hovland et al. (1953) at Yale University, it emphasises the need to look at the person giving the message, the content of the message and the characteristics of the receiver. The Yale model suggests that, first, the message must be listened to (attention), then it must be understood (comprehension), then it must be accepted (acceptance), and finally it must be remembered (retention). These four processes lead to successful persuasion (and a change in attitude). Hovland and colleagues studied these processes and found that various factors affected whether the communication was successful or not. Persuasive speakers are good communicators and the message is likely to be believed more if the communicator is:

- an expert
- a rapid speaker
- giving the message in a subtle way (as if not intended to persuade)
- talking to people with low self-esteem or to people who might feel inferior to the speaker
- giving a message that involves fear
- similar in some way to the person receiving the message
- popular and attractive

Evaluation

- The Yale studies tended to be experiments and took place in unnatural situations. The messages being communicated were not real and important ones. Therefore, the participants would not have been as involved as recipients of the message as they might have been in their everyday lives, so the findings might not be very secure.
- In any communication there are complex interactions between individuals, whereas in studies such as these, variables are isolated for study, and so the situation is unnatural. For example, we could vary whether a speaker is attractive or not but other factors affecting how the message is received are likely to be present.

Applying the ideas to recycling

Reasons for non-cooperation with regard to environmentally friendly behaviour, and ways of changing attitudes to lead to more responsible behaviour (in environmental terms), can be applied to particular issues such as recycling and reclamation. Recycling

involves reusing the same resource; reclamation is using waste material again but for a different product. Recycling and reclamation are forms of resource recovery. There may be an official policy to separate any waste that is dumped and to reuse as much as possible. This does not involve a change in attitude of individuals but it is an expensive option and funding for such action comes from individuals (as taxpayers).

The emphasis in many countries now is on persuading individuals to help in the resource recovery process. To increase recycling behaviour in individuals there is a need to improve understanding of environmental issues and to change attitudes. Gifford (1997) suggests that 70 000 trees would be saved in 1 year if the recycling rate of one community of 200 000 people was 68%. This sort of information can help to persuade people to recycle. Surveys suggest that 81% of students (Williams, 1991) and 58% of householders (Oskamp et al., 1991) report recycling. Lansana (1992) suggests that those who have more understanding of environmental issues recycle more, and this is evidence for the earlier claim that knowledge of issues increases environmentally friendly behaviour.

A system of rewards and punishments can increase environmentally friendly behaviour, as can successful communication of a message. Various studies have found that information works — whether communication is by leaflet or personal message (e.g. DeYoung et al., 1993). Burn (1991) used neighbourhood leaders to approach others to encourage recycling, and this personal approach was more successful than written requests. It has also been found that positive reinforcement works (e.g. Lord, 1994).

Positive reinforcement in conjunction with persuasion works too. Witmer and Geller (1976) found that when leaflets were delivered to all students living in two dormitories once a week there was more recycling behaviour. Alongside the leaflets, they used two reward systems. One reward was a prize for the best dormitory, and this led to around 250 kg of paper being recycled each week. The second reward system used raffle tickets with more prizes and this yielded around 370 kg of paper a week. It seems that the leaflets worked, but they worked better with a reward system, and the higher reward led to better results.

Evaluation

+ Studies with a practical application, such as those looking at improving recycling behaviour, clearly have value to society.
– Although rewards seem to improve recycling behaviour, once the reward is removed the behaviour tends to revert to the original level.
– Reward systems in studies are not too costly to set up as they are small scale. However, on a large scale, reward systems are unlikely to be cost effective.

Application C: Health psychology

Health and substance abuse

Terms that you need to be able to define are given in Table 10.

Table 10 Substance abuse terms

Term	Definition
Substance abuse	Use of a substance other than for its original purpose, e.g. glue itself is not harmful but it is harmful when abused or misused. Use of drugs becomes abuse when someone cannot stop taking the substance, and when problems in general functioning arise due to use of the substance.
Psychological dependence	A compulsion to take a substance, even if not physiologically dependent upon it. Psychological dependence on a substance is when it helps a person feel good and to live his/her life. Heroin and cocaine are likely to lead to psychological dependence; LSD is less likely to.
Physiological dependence	Use of a substance to maintain normal functioning of the body. Heroin is likely to lead to physiological dependence; LSD is not likely to. Physiological dependence tends to follow on from psychological dependence.
Tolerance	The capacity to endure the effects of a substance, especially after it has been taken over a long period. As part of physiological dependence, the body increasingly adapts to a substance and then needs more of it to have the same effect until at some stage a plateau is reached.
Withdrawal	Symptoms experienced when someone is physiologically and/or psychologically dependent on a substance and then stops using it. These symptoms are often short-lived, but very unpleasant. They include headaches, cravings, shaking and feelings of anxiety.
Relapse	When someone manages to stop using a substance but then starts using it again.
Abstinence	The act of not using a substance to which there was previously addiction. During abstinence, there can be withdrawal symptoms.
Addiction	Compulsive psychological and/or physiological dependence on a substance.

Neurotransmitters, synaptic functioning and drugs

Some drugs trigger a neurotransmitter message while others prevent or inhibit synaptic functioning. Examples of drugs that inhibit the message are those used as local anaesthetics. Drugs that block the effect of a neurotransmitter are called 'antagonists'; drugs that increase the effect of a neurotransmitter are called 'agonists'.

Note that the neurotransmitter released at the terminal button must be the right one, or one very similar in 'shape', or the message will not travel on. This is very important as drugs often mimic certain naturally occurring neurotransmitters, but there is not an exact match. This can cause damage at the synapse. The same neurotransmitter can have a different effect on different neurones. Serotonin, dopamine and adrenaline are three well-known neurotransmitters.

Some examples of so-called 'recreational drugs' and how they link to neurotransmitters are given in Table 11.

Table 11 Drugs and neurotransmitter functioning

Drug	Effects on neurotransmitter functioning
Amphetamine	• Blocks the reuptake of dopamine and noradrenaline, so the neurotransmitters are effective for longer (they remain in the synaptic gap to be received) • Increases the release of noradrenaline • Dopamine and noradrenaline increase alertness
Cannabis	• May influence serotonin • Small amounts have a sedative effect, but a high intake can cause greater sensitivity
Angel dust (PCP)	• Blocks serotonin receptors from receiving serotonin, which means a person feels distanced from reality and more peaceful • Serotonin is linked to sleep
Cocaine	• Acts like amphetamine, and is addictive • Increases activity by increasing dopamine and noradrenaline

Effects of alcohol

In 1992, men aged 16 and over were drinking on average 15.9 units per week (General Household Survey). Women were drinking a third of this, at 5.4 units per week. Around 27% of men and 11% of women were drinking more than the recommended maximum. According to the Department of Health, the safe amount is 21 units for men and 14 units for women. In 2002, males aged 16 and over were drinking 17.2 units per week and females 7.6 units per week (General Household Survey).

Behavioural effects

Alcohol makes people less inhibited. It can bring about cognitive deficits such as memory loss or differences in attention ability, and can affect an individual's movements.

Physiological effects

Alcohol interferes with activity in the neurones. GABA is a neurotransmitter that inhibits messages. GABA receptors are made more active by alcohol, so the consumption of alcohol causes messages to be inhibited. The reduction in action potentials results in relaxation and less anxiety (people are calmer). If regular, heavy drinkers abstain from alcohol use, they experience withdrawal symptoms.

Why are some people more affected than others?

It seems likely that genetic factors are involved, at least to some extent. For example, individuals from families in which someone has/had a drink problem are more likely to develop a drink problem themselves, even if they are brought up apart from that person (Gabrielli and Plomin, 1985). One gene is found more often in drug abusers than non-drug abusers (Smith et al., 1992) and this gene is also found in 69% of alcoholics compared with 20% of non-alcoholics.

Evaluation

+ This is strong evidence for there being a genetic cause.
+ The evidence is strong because of the use of control groups. For example, alcoholics were compared with non-alcoholics, and in the other study, some of those with alcoholic relatives lived apart from their family, so a genetic cause can be claimed.
– Even though there seems to be a genetic factor in addiction, it is likely that there are other causes.

Tip

This is a useful topic for discussing the 'nature/nurture' issue (Unit 6).

Long-term effects

Cognitive impairment is common in those who drink alcohol and there can be permanent damage if the drinking is long term. Memory in particular can be affected. Problems with motor performance, such as difficulty in walking and shaking of the limbs, may become noticeable and permanent over time. Long-term drinking can lead to cirrhosis of the liver. Liver cells are replaced by scar tissue, the liver cannot function properly and the blood cannot be cleansed. Heavy drinking (long term) has been linked to heart disease, cancer, high blood pressure and brain damage.

The above effects are all negative, but some research suggests that drinking a little is good for the individual (e.g. Rimm et al., 1991). Research carried out for the Department of Health (1995) found that 1–2 units per day could protect against coronary heart disease (CHD).

Effects of abstinence

The effects of abstinence depend on the length of time of the abuse. Some damage from long-term use of alcohol will not improve with abstinence. For example, liver damage, memory disruption and shaking of the limbs may be permanent. However, physical damage can repair over time, and some effects are reversible. If the abuse of alcohol has not been too long term, permanent damage is unlikely to have occurred.

Effects of nicotine

Physical effects

A 1990 survey suggested that 33% of men and 30% of women in the UK smoked (Office of Population, Censuses and Surveys, 1990). By 2002, the figures were 27% of men and 25% of women, and these figures had been stable for a decade. Men smoked

15 cigarettes a day on average and women 13 cigarettes a day (General Household Survey). Nicotine is both a stimulant and a relaxant. It stimulates the heart rate and blood pressure, and can either stimulate breathing or slow it down. Nicotine stimulates the neuromuscular junction of skeletal muscles and one type of acetylcholine receptor (the nicotinic receptor) found in the central nervous system. If the nicotinic receptor is blocked (if acetylcholine is not received), paralysis results, so stimulating it has the opposite effect. Nicotine also stimulates dopamine receptors, increasing alertness, heart rate and blood pressure, but it can affect people in different ways.

Cigarette smoke contains carbon monoxide, which is absorbed into the bloodstream and reduces the oxygen-carrying capacity of the blood. Smoking is linked to coronary heart disease; in 1993 the Department of Health suggested that 18% of deaths from CHD were caused by smoking cigarettes.

Psychological effects

Schachter et al. (1977) found that smokers smoked more cigarettes when they were limited to low-nicotine cigarettes than they did when they were allowed high-nicotine cigarettes. This suggests that they smoked for the nicotine rather than by habit or other social reasons. This may have been to avoid withdrawal symptoms. Some smokers, however, might smoke to relax, or because nicotine, as a stimulant, causes them to be more alert. These are psychological, not physiological, reasons for smoking.

Long-term effects

Most people associate smoking cigarettes with the development of cancer, particularly lung cancer. Stepney (1982) discussed two studies that support the claim that cigarette smoking causes cancer. One study found that non-smokers live longer than those who smoke; the other study found that when animals are given cigarette tar they develop cancer.

Evaluation

+ It is now generally accepted, from findings of studies such as those mentioned above, that chemicals in tobacco do cause cancer.
– It is not straightforward to claim that findings from studies on animals relate to humans.
– Finding a link between two things, such as cigarette smoking and cancer, is a long way from saying that one causes the other. Other factors may be involved and finding a correlation between two variables is not the same as linking cause to effect.

Effects of abstinence

Smokers who give up report immediate benefits, such as feeling fitter and more energetic as well as having fewer colds. If smoking has caused lung cancer or any other form of cancer, then clearly abstinence at that stage will make no difference. However, it appears to take up to 30 years for lung cancer to develop from smoking, so giving up smoking even after 20 years can be beneficial. Sandvik et al. (1995) found that men who gave up smoking showed lung function performance as good as those who had never smoked.

It is thought that smoking affects men more than women, but this could be because it takes a long time for the effects of smoking to occur. Women (historically) took up smoking later than men did, so the effects on women may be the same but are only recently becoming clear.

Factors of addiction

Tip

Recall the learning approach that you studied at AS. Take a few moments to note down how learning theories could explain addiction. Consider social learning theory and modelling, classical conditioning and operant conditioning.

Learning theory explanations for addictive behaviour

Social learning theory is one explanation for addiction. It suggests that we model ourselves on those around us. Some people may take drugs — and not be able to stop — because they are influenced by those around them, or by other models such as celebrities. Young people are more likely to smoke if their parents or those around them smoke, and this is evidence that some sort of social learning is taking place.

Evaluation

- If smoking runs in families, there could be a genetic explanation.

Operant conditioning can also explain addiction. It is claimed that some people drink alcohol because it helps them to relax in social situations. As they relax and feel better in such situations, this is pleasant and reinforces the need for alcohol. They might then drink so that the pleasurable feeling is repeated. This is the law of effect — if the effect is pleasant, then the behaviour is repeated. When a behaviour is repeated because of pleasant consequences, this is positive reinforcement. Similarly, some drugs give feelings of euphoria, and these would be positive reinforcers. Negative reinforcement is when a behaviour is repeated to avoid unpleasant consequences. If someone takes a drug such as heroin to avoid withdrawal symptoms, this is negative reinforcement.

Evaluation

- Drugs do not always give a positive experience. Yet drugs are still taken. So operant conditioning is unlikely to be the only explanation, even though it can explain some drug-taking behaviour.

Cognitive explanations

Cognitive factors, such as self-esteem, may be involved in drug-taking behaviour. This is similar to the explanation offered by operant conditioning. If something makes people feel better, they are likely to continue with that behaviour. Raising one's self-esteem tends to lead to a more positive outlook, so the behaviour that leads to this raised self-esteem is likely to be repeated. Expectations about the effect(s) of taking

the drug might affect behaviour too. However, there are other cognitive factors to take into account, such as whether people see the drug as harmful or not, as this might outweigh any positive effects. These issues are considered by the health belief model and the theory of reasoned action.

Social explanations

Social factors that help to explain addictive behaviour link closely to the explanation provided by social learning theory. People tend to conform to social norms and will tend to model their behaviour on that of those around them. Significant others (those that we are likely to model ourselves on) include parents and peers.

Evidence for the importance of social factors in explaining addictive behaviour comes from social learning theory and related studies, and also from looking at other cultures where different behaviour is found. If different behaviour is exhibited in other cultures, then we can assume that such behaviour is caused socially rather than biologically.

Studies show a link between social class, income and alcohol consumption. Blaxter (1990) found that alcohol consumption is closely related to other unhealthy behaviours such as smoking, especially in young, working-class males. Power et al. (1991) suggested that young men from lower social classes are more likely to suffer poor health from alcohol consumption than young professional men. However, we should not forget that genetic factors may be involved in addictive behaviour. Social factors seem to be implicated in all drug taking. It is not, of course, that these are causal factors. Other factors, such as low self-esteem, low expectations and lack of positive reinforcement from other areas of life, could link with low social class and poor income.

Genetic explanations

Recall what was said about reasons for drinking alcohol, and how it has been suggested that there is a gene for such behaviour. Some people might become addicted to certain behaviours for genetic reasons.

Stress

Definitions

- **Stressor**. Anything that can cause stress — something that we see as harmful or threatening, from noise or heat to major life events.
- **Strain**. The response to a stressor, which can be psychological and/or physiological. First we appraise the situation in a practical sense. We continue to appraise it using whatever information we have, such as how long the stressor is likely to continue, or what we can do about it. Strain is experienced when these appraisals indicate a problem with coping.

- **Stress**. This includes both stressors and strain. It is the whole process of experiencing a stressor and responding to it. Stress is experienced when people perceive themselves as not having the resources needed to deal with a certain situation. The perception of the individual is clearly important.

Stress factors

Stress is likely to involve both internal personality factors and external environmental stressors, both of which trigger physiological reactions. It is probably the case that neither external nor internal factors alone lead to stress but that an interaction occurs. The earlier section on environmental psychology outlined how external stressors can affect individuals, and cited noise and heat as being two examples. Some people are affected by certain environmental features such as excessive noise more than others, so internal factors are also important.

Internal factors

Internal factors include level of self-esteem, motivation of the individual and a person's beliefs about a situation. Those with high self-esteem are less likely to be stressed, as they are more inclined to see themselves as having the required resources to deal with situations. On the other hand, if people are highly motivated to achieve a certain goal, then this can add pressure and can reduce their feelings of competence to achieve that goal. The more people's beliefs match reality, the less likely they are to be stressed. So, having high motivation can lead to stress, whereas having high self-esteem can help to avoid stress, as can having realistic beliefs. Clearly this links to the cognitive approach, and positive thinking together with rational thoughts can help in avoiding stress.

External factors

External factors are environmental aspects. They include how sudden a situation is, whether the situation is a major life event, the timing of such an event, the amount of ambiguity (e.g. role ambiguity), how desirable an event is and the amount of control over the situation that a person has.

If there is little time to deal with a situation rationally or to consider whether your internal resources are sufficient to deal with the demands of a situation, then stress is likely to occur. So sudden situations that need an immediate response are likely to be more stressful than those where there is time to think things through.

Major life events are stressful, probably because resources are needed to cope with them that we don't usually draw upon. These major life events can be more stressful if they occur unexpectedly. Usual life events, even major ones, are expected to an extent, and society can give us ways of coping.

Role ambiguity can also lead to stress. Ambiguity generally means that we cannot easily appraise the situation; thus we cannot judge what resources are needed, so we are more likely to think that we do not have the required resources to deal with the situation.

Desirable events (e.g. weddings, moving house) can be stressful but are usually less stressful than undesirable events. It is possible that desirable events are seen as socially acceptable and so there is social support available. People are more likely to see themselves as having the resources to cope with desirable events.

A situation is often less stressful if people feel they have control over what is happening.

Interactional factors

It is not so much the external factors or events that lead to stress, but how a person deals with the situation. For example, a desirable event can be less stressful than an undesirable one, and whether a situation is desirable or not depends on internal factors — at least to an extent. There is an interaction between the external event — how sudden it is, the timing of the event and what type of event it is — and the internal reaction — whether there is time to work out what resources are needed to cope with the situation and whether the situation can be viewed as desirable.

Physiological responses to stress and effects on the immune system

The alarm reaction

Stress is an internal reaction in the sense that it is physiological. The alarm reaction, sometimes called the 'fight or flight response', is a physiological response to a sudden situation. It is a useful survival trait; in a threatening situation, we can draw on reserves either to fight or run away. Evolution has prepared us to react to threatening situations in this way, and this is not stress as such; it is a normal and useful reaction. However, our bodies sometimes maintain this reaction, and drawing on reserves for the energy needed can leave us vulnerable and weak. If our bodies maintain this reaction beyond the immediate situation, we are unable to sustain the level of energy needed and this causes stress and strain.

Physiological changes

The autonomic nervous system (ANS) comprises the sympathetic and the parasympathetic nervous systems. The sympathetic nervous system prepares the body for action by means of the alarm reaction. The parasympathetic nervous system restores equilibrium and gets things back to normal. Stress occurs when normality is not resumed — when the parasympathetic nervous system has not done its work. Information (from the outside world), processed via the cortex and the hypothalamus, triggers the sympathetic nervous system into action. The sympathetic nervous system, through the adrenal glands (and the pituitary gland), leads to the secretion of corticosteroids, which increase access to body energy stores and inhibit antibody formation. According to Sarafino (1994), the adrenal glands secrete hormones; stressors such as noise, pain and crowding increase this process. The sympathetic nervous system also leads to the secretion of catecholamines (adrenaline and noradrenaline). These increase blood pressure, heart rate and breathing rate, slow digestion and divert blood to the muscle tissue.

A continued state of arousal, that is, if the alarm reaction is maintained, can do us harm. For example, increased levels of cortisol can destroy cells in the hippocampus and so affect memory. If excessive levels of adrenaline and noradrenaline are maintained, blood pressure and heart rate remain high and the immune system can be affected.

Evaluation

- There is no simple explanation for the physiological changes involved in stress; complex factors are at work. For example, not only do environmental stressors lead to the physiological response that is strain, but other factors, such as the type of person (internal factors), are also involved. The amount of emotion is also important.

Effects on the immune system

Increases in cortisol can impact adversely on the immune system by affecting lymphocyte functioning. Lymphocytes are white blood cells that destroy antigens (foreign substances). The immune system can be measured by seeing how lymphocytes divide, because this is what happens when the immune system functions properly. Alternatively, the number of helper T-cells and natural killer (NK) cells can be counted. These measures show that stress and a weakened immune system are linked (e.g. Cohen and Herbert, 1996).

The general adaptation syndrome (GAS) is the pattern of bodily response seen when the alarm reaction continues after the parasympathetic nervous system should have cancelled it. First, the alarm reaction occurs. Then there is resistance as the arousal level is maintained because the body perceives itself as still under threat. Remember that stress occurs when we think we do not have the resources to cope with the situation. The body is most vulnerable at the resistance stage because energy is used to renew the hormones released by the adrenal glands. Likely health problems at this stage include ulcers, high blood pressure and asthma. Finally, exhaustion occurs when resources to maintain the alarm reaction become limited. By this stage the immune system is very low.

Factors that may cause stress

A biological factor: disruption of circadian rhythms

We have several biological rhythms. Disruptions to the sleep/wake cycle, such as occur during shiftwork, can cause stress.

Tip

Recall your AS material on bodily rhythms and how disruption of these, for example through shift work or jet-lag, can lead to physiological problems.

A social factor: lack of social support

Unemployment and retirement are social situations that can be more or less stressful according to the amount of social support involved for the individual. When people receive social support, they are comforted, helped and cared for by others. Lynch

(1977) found that married people live longer, and this could be because they can give each other social support in all situations. Arnetz et al. (1987) compared unemployed people on benefits and found that those on a psychosocial support programme showed better immune functioning. This suggests that lack of social support can cause stress. However, it could be that social support helps to alleviate stress, which is not quite the same thing. The 'direct effect' hypothesis says that lack of support is actually stressful, whereas the 'stress buffering' hypothesis suggests that it is the social support that helps to alleviate stress.

A psychological factor: emotion

The types and levels of hormones released by the adrenal glands depend on the levels of emotion felt. High emotion tends to involve the release of adrenaline, noradrenaline and cortisol, whereas lower emotion can mean only two of these are released. The type of emotion can affect the level of stress too. Fear gives rise to stress, as might be expected given the role of the 'fight or flight' response. Depression is also linked to stress. Illnesses that are associated with stress, for example those that affect the heart, lungs and blood pressure, or those related to the immune system, can be linked with depression. Note also that stress occurs when people feel they do not have the necessary resources to cope with a certain situation. There is clearly a role here for cognitive factors such as self-efficacy and self-esteem.

Coping strategies

Defence mechanisms

Recall material from the psychodynamic approach — in particular Freud's explanation of defence mechanisms.

One way of protecting ourselves is to repress unwanted emotions into our unconscious. Through repression, any thoughts that may make us anxious are kept out of our conscious mind. Another defence mechanism is denial — where we ignore something that makes us anxious by denying its existence or by explaining it away. Repression and denial mean that we do not have to admit to ourselves that we feel we do not have the resources to cope with a situation. We either deny that there is a problem or repress our anxiety altogether. So it could be said that by using defence mechanisms we are coping with an otherwise stressful situation. Of course, we do not consciously use defence mechanisms. If this were a conscious process, it would not work. The whole point is to keep thoughts buried in the unconscious. Defence mechanisms are a useful strategy if there is nothing we can do about a situation or if problem-focusing does not work. However, if something can be done, then it is better to focus on the problem.

Problem-focused strategies

Stress occurs when we feel we do not have the resources to cope with a particular situation. Problem-focused strategies involve altering the situation or changing the available resources to enable us to cope. For example, if a job is stressful, we can solve the problem by leaving the post or by finding out how to deal with certain aspects of the job more effectively — perhaps by going on a course. When the situation and/or the resource can be changed, problem-focused strategies are best.

Emotion-focused strategies

If the situation itself or the available resources cannot be changed, then another way of coping with stress is to focus on feelings. Feelings can be changed by practical means such as taking medication or by getting social support from others. We can try to change our feelings by changing our thinking or our perception of a situation. We could think of worse things that could happen, or focus on any positive aspect of a stressful situation. Another mechanism for altering emotions involves avoiding them by denying that something is happening. Hence it can be seen that defence mechanisms are a form of emotion focusing. Lazarus and Folkman (1948) suggest that when a situation cannot be changed, emotion focusing is best.

Evaluation

- ± Problem focusing is best if a situation or the resources for coping with it can be changed. Otherwise emotion focusing or defence mechanisms are best.
- ± Other factors affect which means of coping is likely to be used. Husbands and wives both use problem-focused strategies but wives use more emotion focusing than husbands (Billings and Moos, 1981). So gender is a factor, as are some social factors such as low income and low education, both of which tend to lead to more emotion focusing.
- ± The type of problem can also guide the type of coping strategy. A death in the family tends to lead to fewer problem-focused strategies, as would be expected, since emotion focusing is more successful in situations that cannot be changed.
- ± Most people use a combination of problem focusing and emotion focusing. For example, you could argue with your boss about your workload to relieve your emotions and at the same time arrange for someone else to take some of the work from you.

Two resources in coping

Social factors

One important resource when coping with stress is social support. Stress can be alleviated, to a certain extent, by support from others. Social support can have a direct effect on coping with stress (the 'direct effect hypothesis'). The 'buffering effect hypothesis' suggests that social support can help to alleviate stress and can protect the individual to an extent. Being able to talk to someone else who has had a similar experience is particularly valuable. Organisations such as Cancer Link and the Stillbirth and Neonatal Death Association were formed to offer such support.

There are four forms of social support. Emotional support is where the individual is comforted and offered a sense of belonging. Esteem support involves giving encouragement and boosting the individual's sense of worth and self-esteem.

Informational support offers advice and guidance. Instrumental support is where practical assistance is offered, such as giving someone a lift to a hospital appointment.

Other social factors include whether the stressor is predictable and how controllable it is. These issues are discussed in the section on environmental psychology (see pp. 51–52). A potential stressor such as noise has more effect if it is unpredictable or if it is not controllable. Uncertainty makes it difficult to deal with a stressful event.

Personal factors

Personal factors, such as individual appraisal of the situation, affect the experience of a situation. Self-esteem and coping skills are also important. There are gender differences in choosing coping strategies: women are likely to choose both emotion-focused and problem-focused strategies, whereas men are more likely to use only problem-focused strategies. There also seem to be cultural differences, as well as age differences, in coping with stress. For example, Ruch and Holmes (1971) found that adolescents rated sexual difficulties as the fifth most stressful item from a list, whereas older adults rated this as item 13. Individual differences are also important. Many people cope with stressful situations without becoming ill, whereas others are much more affected. Sarafino (1994) suggests that a person's scores on life events, as measured by traditional scales, do not correlate with that person's illnesses. In addition, correlations do not show cause and effect. For example, a person may be ill not because of stress over a death in the family but because of not eating properly following such an event.

Health promotion

Preventive medicine and health education programmes aim to reduce illness, and to improve people's knowledge of how to maintain health. Health promotion aims to change morbidity (the incidence of a disease) and mortality (the prevalence of the disease as well as the numbers of people dying from it).

Preventive healthcare

Caplan (1969) suggested that there are three levels of preventive healthcare: primary prevention, secondary prevention and tertiary prevention.

Evaluation

+ Caplan's ideas can be applied to health promotion as much as to prevention of ill health.
+ Some prevention campaigns, such as immunisation programmes, have been so successful that infectious diseases such as tuberculosis, diphtheria and smallpox have been almost eradicated in the Western world. Current concerns have affected the take-up of the MMR vaccine. Health promotion campaigns are not the only literature available and other factors can affect people's attitudes and behaviour.

- Caplan's ideas are based on the medical model and if it is thought that ill health can be prevented, then clearly the underlying assumption is that ill health comes from sociobiological sources. However, Caplan was originally looking at mental health in the community when talking about prevention, and wanted to focus on the potential of people to solve their problems in a reality based way.
- When focusing on prevention, health becomes simply the absence of disease, whereas it might be seen by many as being more than this, and as being something positive in its own right.
- Focusing on prevention can suggest that health professionals know best, and that individuals cannot be trusted to look after themselves. This view can seem to blame those who become ill. As there can be social and environmental causes for ill health, this idea of blaming the victim is a narrow view.

Primary prevention

The first level of preventive care is primary prevention, which involves reducing the risk of people becoming ill. Examples of primary prevention include the immunisation programme for children, the prevention of pregnancy by contraception and the prevention of injury and death on the roads by promoting the use of seat belts.

Evaluation

+ Although people do not act just on knowledge from a government programme, without such knowledge they are less likely to engage in health promoting behaviours.
- Factors other than the message from a health promotion programme can affect an individual's attitudes. People hold beliefs from other sources too. For example, some girls believe that they cannot get pregnant 'the first time'. Peer pressure can also affect health behaviour.
- Alderson et al. (1997) studied parents and their decisions regarding immunisation. They found that doctors gave detailed information to try to persuade parents to engage in health promoting actions, and offered encouragement and reassurance, and listened to parents, to help them make what the doctors considered to be the right decision. So health promotion campaigns on their own may not be enough.
- People may resist health promoting behaviours owing to a lack of knowledge or confidence. There can also be practical reasons, such as lacking the means to get to a clinic. There seems to be a lower uptake of immunisation among families in lower socioeconomic groups. Blackburn (1991) found that such families have the same health goals for their families, even though their behaviour is different. She suggested that the inequality in uptake of such programmes arose from inequalities in income and situation, rather than different attitudes and beliefs.

Secondary prevention

Secondary prevention involves attempting to reduce the prevalence of a disorder and the length of time it lasts. The emphasis is on early diagnosis and effective treatment. An example of secondary prevention is the monitoring of people with high blood pressure to reduce strokes. Screening programmes also represent secondary

prevention as they aim to diagnose an illness and treat it early enough to be successful. One secondary prevention programme involved a government aim to reduce the incidence of invasive cervical cancer by at least 20% by the year 2000. The NHS now offers women aged 20–65 a smear test every 5 years to screen for cervical cancer. In 2002, 81.6% of women aged 25–64 were screened. So there is more to prevention than screening, but screening does appear to give more of a chance of treatment and therefore preventing death. There is no primary prevention programme because there are no clear risk factors, so no health promotion campaign can be mounted. However, it has been suggested that risk factors associated with cervical cancer include smoking, the number of sexual partners, the contraceptive pill and the papilloma virus, so it might be that a primary prevention campaign will be mounted soon.

Evaluation

- Mant (1994) suggested that some doctors are concerned that there are programmes to discover problems before there are effective treatment programmes available.
- Screening programmes depend on cost–benefit analysis. They are only mounted if the likely benefits outweigh the costs.
- The success of secondary prevention programmes like screening depends on acceptance by the general public. If they are not accepted, they will not be worthwhile because the uptake will be too low.

Tertiary prevention

Tertiary prevention includes rehabilitation services, which aim to prevent further disability and to alleviate suffering. An example of tertiary prevention is the control of pain.

Health education programmes

Health education programmes aim to achieve changes in morbidity and mortality of a disease. They focus on reducing the incidence of a disease (morbidity) and on reducing its consequences (its spread and effect). Health education programmes are primary prevention programmes.

HIV/AIDS and smoking

One health education programme focuses on acquired immune deficiency syndrome (AIDS) and the human immunodeficiency virus (HIV). Government literature printed in newspapers and magazines is there as a reminder of the number of people who are HIV positive and the number who die from AIDS. Figures are also given that predict future numbers if we do not change our sexual behaviour. The aim is to persuade people not to engage in unsafe sex and not to use intravenous drugs (where needles are shared). Individual and group counselling is offered as part of the campaign. It is easy to show the negative side of engaging in unsafe sex — there is no cure for AIDS and visual aspects of the illness can be shown. However, there are still difficulties in persuading people that it can happen to them; the health belief model outlined below can help to explain these difficulties. Arousing fear in people with frightening messages is not always the best way to change attitudes, but information is important.

For example, if heterosexuals think that AIDS and HIV are only contracted by homosexuals, then they are unlikely to be affected by campaigns regarding safe sex.

Some campaigns focus on changing attitudes, others on changing habits. Some campaigns focus on the negative consequences of not changing the undesired behaviour and some emphasise the positive consequences of changing the behaviour. The most effective campaigns embrace both positive and negative factors. For example, with regard to smoking, the benefits include feeling more healthy and having more energy, as well as saving money and not having to be antisocial at work by going outside to smoke. Negative aspects to smoking include having less money and finding it harder to socialise (these days), and can also include showing people the likely state of their lungs, or giving figures linking smoking to certain diseases.

Most people must now be aware that there is a correlation between smoking and certain illnesses. It is claimed that smoking is a causal factor in many illnesses, such as heart disease and cancer. It is hard to believe that anyone who smokes does not know that there are health risks associated with such behaviour. Cigarette packets display the words 'Smoking kills!'. However, people still smoke, and many start smoking in spite of such campaigns. The health belief model outlined below can help to explain why, in the face of mounting evidence that smoking is implicated in many diseases, people continue to smoke.

Rogers (1990) suggests that a fear-arousing message is not enough by itself. People need to realise that they can do something about the situation. For example, if people think that it is too late to give up smoking to do any good, they are likely to continue. However, if they realise that the effects of smoking can be reversed quite quickly, then they might be persuaded to give up. One simple idea is to get people to change their behaviour for one day. Days such as 'no smoking day' raise awareness and encourage people to try. One day might not seem too difficult, and they might then be encouraged to continue. Giving up for a day is an active measure, whereas fear messages are passively received.

Evaluation

± The general evaluation comments concerning primary prevention programmes given above apply here. One issue is that health education programmes do not occur in isolation. People have existing beliefs and they are also affected by other people around them. Another issue is that changing attitudes and behaviour in the light of a health education programme might only be possible for those with funding to do so. People in lower socioeconomic groups seem to engage in less preventive behaviour. This could be because those on a low income do not have the resources to attend clinics.

The health belief model

Health promotion campaigns aim to empower people to reach health decisions. However, educating people is not the only factor in persuading them to make such

decisions. People's beliefs and values are also important. Such issues affect, for example, how the message is received, and are also important in influencing an individual's behaviour. After all, a message can be understood and even accepted (most people accept that smoking is bad for one's health), but this does not mean that an individual obeys the message. There are clearly other factors at work.

Davison et al. (1991) investigated which factors people thought might lead to a heart attack, such as obesity, fatty diet and smoking. Other factors included whether someone was a worrier or bad-tempered. If people do not see themselves as falling into these categories, they are not likely to engage in preventive behaviour.

Becker and Maiman (1975) discussed the health belief model. The idea was to explain, by using a model, why some people do not carry out health preventive action. They suggested various obstacles that would prevent such behaviour, including the individual's perceived susceptibility to disease, the perceived severity of the disease and the perceived threat. The health belief model suggests that someone will weigh the perceived benefits of preventive action against the perceived barriers, taking various factors into account. Social factors such as age, social class, race and ethnicity also seem to be important. So people look at how likely they are to get the disease, and how severe it is likely to be if they do. If it seems unlikely to them that they will become ill, then the perceived threat is low. They will look at the benefits of the preventive action and what it will involve. If it is a lot of trouble (e.g. exercising every day), and they don't think they are in a group that is at risk of the disease, then they will probably choose not to undertake the preventive action. If they perceive themselves as being likely to get the disease (e.g. because family members have developed it), then the cost of the preventive measures might not seem so high.

The health belief model suggests that there are two main factors that lead to people engaging in health-promoting behaviour, or not. One factor is their belief in the health threat; the other is their belief that specific behaviour can reduce the threat. They will weigh these two things up, as outlined above.

When discussing whether people indulge in health-related behaviours, it is often primary prevention that is being discussed, such as whether someone will take necessary exercise. However, people also weigh up the pros and cons of secondary preventive behaviours, such as whether to attend an appointment for a test or whether to take medication to keep blood pressure low. Even with tertiary preventive behaviour, where it would be thought that reducing pain and prolonging life would be welcomed by all, people can still decide whether to accept certain types of treatment or not. This may depend on their beliefs about the situation.

Evaluation

- The health belief model does not account for simple health-related behaviour, such as cleaning one's teeth.
- The health belief model does not take into account the views of others.

The theory of reasoned action

The theory of reasoned action differs from the health belief model in that it emphasises the decision-making part of the process. Ajzen and Fishbein (1980) claimed that if we know people's intentions, then we can better predict what they will do, and that we do act according to our intentions. As with the health belief model, the theory of reasoned action suggests that people's beliefs about the outcome of any action will affect their intentions. If they think the outcome will be rewarding, then their intentions are likely to differ from their intentions if they think the outcome will be negative. As well as their beliefs about the behaviour (whether it will work or not, for example), other people's opinions are important, and this is where the theory of reasoned action differs from the health belief model. The theory of reasoned action suggests that people's intentions about their health-related behaviour are affected by other people's responses to that behaviour. For example, if the behaviour is not socially acceptable, they are not likely to engage in it, whereas if it is socially acceptable (e.g. giving up smoking), then they are more likely to engage in it.

So the intention as to whether to engage in health-related behaviour is governed not only by whether the individual thinks that such behaviour will work and would be useful, but also by whether other people engage in such behaviour and whether those around think it is acceptable. The main difference between the health belief model and the theory of reasoned action is the emphasis on social norms.

Evaluation

- Intentions do not always predict actions. Many people intend to give up smoking, but do not. Even when they know the health risks, their family is in favour of them giving up and society disapproves of smoking, they still smoke.
- Previous experiences affect behaviour too and these are not included in the theory.

Questions & Answers

The questions that follow are similar to those you will meet in the exam. Research Methods questions are given first, followed by ones on the three Applications (child, environmental and health psychology). You should only look at the questions on the Application that you have studied.

Research methods

Two questions (worth a total of 36 marks) are presented in the same format as the actual unit test. In the examination you should expect at least one question that gives a scenario/study and then asks questions based on this stimulus material. There is likely to be another question with a slightly more general focus.

Applications

The Applications Questions are exam-style questions, but note that they are not presented as they would be in an exam paper. Note the following points about Applications Questions:

- There is often stimulus material to put you in the right frame of reference for the question. It takes you to the right area in your studies and helps to set the scene. Read the material with this purpose in mind.
- Sometimes the stimulus material must be referred to in your answer. The question will make this clear. If this is the case, make sure you mention something about the stimulus material at least once in your answer, otherwise you will not get full marks.
- Look out for questions asking you to describe a study. Remember to give the aim, method, results and conclusion and not, for example, just the method or the results.
- Note the number of marks available for each question. If there are two tasks and 8 marks available, expect there to be 4 marks for each part of the question.
- Remember the marking strategy for essays. Allow 2 marks for clarity and communication, 2 marks for balance and breadth, and divide the other marks equally between AO1 (knowledge with understanding) and AO2 (evaluation and comment).
- Although there are three sections in the specification for each of the Applications and three main questions, it is not necessarily the case that there will be one question from each section.

Examiner's comments

All questions and answers are followed by examiner's comments. These are preceded by the icon e. They indicate where credit is due and point out areas for improvement, specific problems and common errors such as poor time management, lack of clarity, weak or non-existent development, irrelevance, misinterpretation of the question and mistaken meanings of terms.

Methodology I

Question 1

A field study was carried out to look at the effect of temperature on helpfulness. Researchers decided that helpfulness would be measured as whether a participant agreed to be interviewed or not. Temperature was measured using a thermometer. The study was carried out in England in February and again in May of the same year. On both occasions, the same same small town was used and the same procedure was followed. The researchers approached individuals on the High Street on a Saturday morning and asked them to complete a survey about holidays. They selected every sixth person they met. The researchers noted whether the person agreed to help or not. They also recorded the temperature each time. They chose a cold but sunny February day and a warm, sunny May morning. It was found that people were more helpful in warm conditions.

(a) Write an alternative hypothesis for the above study. (2 marks)

(b) What is the independent variable (IV)? (1 mark)

(c) What is the dependent variable (DV)? (1 mark)

(d) What is the level of measurement of the dependent variable (DV)? (1 mark)

(e) Describe *one* control that the researchers carefully put in place. (4 marks)

(f) Outline *one* strength and *one* weakness of operationalising helpfulness as whether someone is willing to undertake an interview or not. (4 marks)

(g) Give a definition of random sampling. (2 marks)

(h) Explain why the sampling used in this study was not random sampling. (2 marks)

(i) Outline *one* problem with the way the participants were chosen. (2 marks)

(j) What inferential statistical test could be used to test the findings? (1 mark)

(k) Give *two* reasons for this being a suitable test. (2 marks)

e **(a)** Avoid giving a null hypothesis — this question clearly asks for an alternative hypothesis. 2 marks are available for a clear hypothesis. Just 1 mark would be awarded if the IV and DV were not both well expressed.

(b) You need to be able to identify the IV and the DV in any study, so practise. Note whether it is the IV or the DV that is asked for. Under exam pressure it is easy to make a mistake, so read the question carefully and underline key words. There is 1 mark for the identification but note that usually there are two parts to the IV and you should give both, for example whether words are categorised or not.

(c) Once you have given the IV you should be able to identify the DV quite easily. It is a good idea to find both the IV and the DV, even if only one is asked for, so that you can be sure you have got it right.

(d) This question asks about levels of measurement. You need to know what these are, so find a way to remember them.

(e) When a variable feature is kept the same over the various conditions of the IV, this is called a control. Controls are used in most studies. Choose one control from the study and explain what it is and how it works. 1 mark is likely

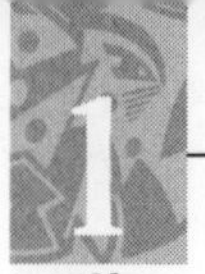

to be for identifying the control itself, and a further 3 marks for expanding and explaining.

(f) When a researcher chooses how to turn an IV or a DV into something that can actually be done and measured, this is called 'operationalising'. You need to give one reason why this way of measuring helpfulness is a good idea and make clear why it is a good idea. Then give one reason why it is not a good way of measuring helpfulness and make clear why it is not. There are 2 marks for the strength and 2 marks for the weakness.

(g) Make sure your definition is thorough, otherwise you are likely to get only 1 of the 2 marks available.

(h) Identify what type of sampling was used in the study and say why it is not random.

(i) Give one difficulty with this method of sampling. Make sure that your answer to **(h)** focuses on why the method is not random and your answer to **(i)** focuses on what the problem is.

(j) You need to know eight inferential tests for this examination. Consider all eight and decide which is most suitable here. Use a flowchart to make your choice.

(k) When choosing the test for **(j)** you will make some decisions such as whether the design is repeated measures or independent groups, and whether the study involves a correlation or not. Choose two of the decisions you have made and write them down here. 1 mark is available for each reason.

Answers to question 1

(a) There is a difference in the number of participants who agree to be interviewed depending on whether the temperature is warm or fairly cold. ✓✓

e This answer scores 2 marks. Helpfulness is measured as agreement to be interviewed, which is how the DV is operationalised (so the DV is correct), and the IV is also correct (warm or fairly cold temperature). Note that this hypothesis is two-tailed as it does not say whether people will be more or less helpful if the weather is warm. A one-tailed hypothesis would be just as good for this answer. For example, you could say that 'participants are more likely to agree to be interviewed when the weather is warm than when it is fairly cold'.

(b) Whether the study is carried out in February or May, that is, whether the weather is fairly cold or warm. ✓

e This is a thorough answer, which gets 1 mark. You could just mention warm or fairly cold conditions. The point is the weather and not the month.

(c) Whether participants agreed to be interviewed or not. ✓

e This is correct and gains 1 mark. Note that 'helpfulness' is not enough. What is actually measured must be given.

(d) Nominal ✓

e One word is not enough usually, but here it gains the mark. The only data recorded (the DV) are whether the participant is willing to be interviewed or not. Basically you would record 'yes' or 'no'. This is putting data into categories and so the data are nominal.

(e) One control is keeping the place the same. ✓ The researchers used the same town each time, the same place and the same day of the week. ✓ So although the temperature varied, other conditions were the same. The same number and type of people are likely to be shopping on a Saturday morning, ✓ and one town is likely to have a similar type of shopper or visitor on a particular day. ✓

e This answer scores the full 4 marks. 1 mark is for the control. It looks as though more than one control is given, as the same town and the same day are mentioned. However, these cover the same situation, so this is acceptable for one control. With 4 marks available, it is a good idea to choose something broad like this. The main point of a control is to keep factors the same and only vary the IV. This point is mentioned in the answer, which is a good idea.

(f) One good thing about operationalising helpfulness as whether something is agreed to or not is that this can be clearly measured. Someone can record whether a participant said 'yes' or 'no', and even a shake of the head is clear. ✓ Indeed, if people agree, they must stop to complete the interview, so the behaviour is observable, which is what is needed. ✓ One disadvantage is that people might say they will complete the interview and later refuse, or they might complete it and lie. ✓ If they refuse or lie, then although they have 'agreed', they have not been helpful, ✓ and it is helpfulness that is being measured.

e The advantage is clear and the main point is that the behaviour is observable and, therefore, measurable. The advantage gets a mark and the elaboration about saying 'yes' or 'no' or shaking the head gets another mark. The disadvantage is less clear — it seems like two disadvantages (refusing to complete the interview and lying). However, the overall point about agreeing on the one hand but not being helpful on the other is credited. 1 mark is given for this point and another mark is awarded for elaborating about lying or refusing later.

(g) Random sampling occurs when everyone in the chosen population has an equal chance of being chosen. ✓✓ This can be done by putting all the names in a hat, for example.

e This is a good answer, for 2 marks. It is a good idea to learn definitions like this. The main points are 'everyone' and 'equal chance of being chosen'.

(h) In this study, only those in the town on a Saturday can be chosen. ✓ The target population is everyone, and everyone would not be there to be chosen on the particular days when the study took place. ✓ So not everyone in the population has an equal chance of being chosen.

This is a thorough answer, for 2 marks, which refers to the main point of random sampling.

(i) The main problem is that, by choosing every sixth person, the others do not have a chance of being picked and this can cause bias. ✓

This answer needs a little more explanation. An example could help, such as 'if a group of friends passed and were the same age and type of person, only one of them could be chosen, which might give bias'. This answer gets 1 mark only.

(j) A chi-squared test is suitable. ✓

This is an appropriate test and scores a mark. There is no other right answer.

(k) These are nominal data and it is an independent groups design. ✓✓

This is a good answer, for 2 marks. Different participants will agree to be interviewed or not (the same person could not both agree and disagree), so this is an independent groups design. It is not a correlation, as 'yes' or 'no' is not a sliding scale, and the different temperature is claimed to cause the difference in agreement. So the two tests for correlations (Spearman and Pearson) are not suitable. There are three tests for independent groups designs (chi-squared, Mann-Whitney and unrelated *t*) but only one is suitable for nominal data (chi-squared).

This answer scores 21/22 marks.

■ ■ ■

Question 2

(a) Give *three* of the BPS ethical guidelines regarding the use of human participants in psychological research. (3 marks)

(b) Give *three* ethical guidelines that are important when using animals in psychological research. (3 marks)

(c) Using the field study outlined for question 1 above, describe the ethical issues that would have arisen. (4 marks)

(d) Explain how the ethical issues you described in (c) could have been dealt with. (4 marks)

(a) There is a list of BPS ethical guidelines. All you need to do here is to choose three of them and list them, without explanation, for 1 mark each.

(b) Again, there is a list of guidelines for using animals and you need to list three, for 1 mark each.

(c) Here you can give four different ethical points for 1 mark each or two points for 2 marks each. Consider the BPS guidelines and then think about the study. Give an ethical issue that might have been considered or one that might not have been thought about. Make sure you write enough for 4 marks and note that the marks are for the issue, not for relating it to the study.

(d) Make sure you use the same issues as you chose for part **(c)** and make suggestions about what could have been done to make the study ethical in terms of these issues. There are 4 marks available, so make sure you say enough. Any suitable idea will gain credit.

Answers to question 2

(a) Debriefing; ✓ informed consent; ✓ confidentiality ✓

e 3 marks are awarded. There are other suitable guidelines.

(b) Suitable caging; ✓ not using an endangered species; ✓ having a suitably qualified person to make sure the animal does not suffer undue pain ✓

e This scores 3 marks. There are other suitable guidelines.

(c) The study required participants to agree to be interviewed or not — the interview itself was not important. One ethical issue is that the participants might have been asked to undertake an unnecessary interview. ✓ This might put pressure on some participants if they are in a hurry; one ethical guideline is that no harm should come to a participant. ✓ Another ethical issue is that of informed consent. It would not be possible to ask the participants if they minded taking part until they had done so, ✓ as they were simply stopped in the street. ✓

e These two issues gain 2 marks each. There are other possible answers.

(d) The participants did not have to complete the interview. ✓ The researchers could have thanked them for agreeing and explained that this was a piece of research. They could then have explained the purpose of the study. ✓ Most people should be quite happy to be told that the study was about whether people were more willing to help on a warm day — after all, those who stopped would have helped in any case so would feel that they were being kind, which is a good feeling. ✓ Some might have been annoyed at being deceived, but if the whole scenario did not take long, hopefully few would have minded. The debrief should take place even without an interview and would help regarding informed consent ✓ — participants could be asked whether their data could be used. However, it would still be true that there was no informed consent and a main problem would be debriefing those who refused to help.

e 4 marks are easily achieved in this answer, which is thorough and relates well to the study. The two ethical issues given in **(c)** are referred to. It is clear that this candidate understands the issues and has some idea of how to make the study ethical. Note that the different points are carefully explained. This is the right way to answer such a question. Avoid bullet points or short answers.

e **This answer scores 14/14 marks. Overall, the score is 35/36 marks.**

Methodology II

Question 1

Students took part in a study to test whether deeper processing led to better recall. Deeper processing was taken to be when the meaning of the word had to be considered, rather than just visual processing taking place. Recall was based on how many words were recognised from the list they had worked with. Each participant was asked to carry out the same task. There was a list of words to read through and for each word they had to do something different. There were two conditions. Sometimes they had to see whether the word was written in capital letters (visual processing) and sometimes they had to fit the word into a sentence (thinking about the meaning of the word). Each participant then had to pick out the words in the list from among other words. It was clear that participants recognised more words from the list when they had had to think about the meaning. They recognised the least number of words when they had simply looked at each word to see if it was written in capital letters. The scores are given below. A Wilcoxon matched pairs signed ranks test was carried out to see if the difference in the number of words recognised when meaning had been processed was significantly different from the number of words recognised when there was only visual processing. T (the result of doing the Wilcoxon test) = 13.5.

Table showing the number of words recognised in the two conditions (when meaning was processed and when visual processing took place). A total of 20 words was processed by each participant.

Participant number	Meaning of word was processed	Visual processing only
1	15	8
2	8	9
3	9	12
4	12	18
5	14	12
6	13	10
7	10	8
8	17	13
9	11	7
10	15	8
Mean	12.4	10.5
Median	12.5	9.5
Mode	15	8
Range	10	12
Standard deviation	2.91	3.34

(a) Write a null hypothesis for this study. (2 marks)

(b) Identify the independent variable (IV). (1 mark)

(c) Give *two* reasons for using a Wilcoxon matched pairs signed ranks test. (2 marks)

(d) Using the information given below, say whether the null hypothesis can be rejected, and give *two* reasons for your decision. (3 marks)
T must be equal to or less than the critical value to be significant. Note that in this study $N = 10$ and $T = 13.5$. The hypothesis is one-tailed.

Critical values of T for the Wilcoxon matched pairs signed ranks test

	Level of significance for a one-tailed test			
N	0.05	0.025	0.01	0.005
9	8	6	3	2
10	11	8	5	3
11	14	11	7	5

(e) Two standard deviation (SD) figures are given. The SD for the condition where meaning is processed is 2.91 and the SD for the condition involving visual processing is 3.34. Explain why standard deviation is a useful measure when considering the findings of studies in psychology. (4 marks)

(f) Give *two* advantages of using the same participants for each condition. (2 marks)

(g) Outline one disadvantage of using the experimental method in this study. (2 marks)

(h) When an experiment is carried out, it is important to control for various factors. Outline *one* control that should have been implemented in this study. (2 marks)

(i) Describe *one* ethical guideline that should have been followed in this study and explain how it should have been followed. (4 marks)

e **(a)** Note that the null hypothesis is requested, not the experimental hypothesis. Mention both the independent variable (IV) and the dependent variable (DV).

(b) Note that the IV is asked for, not the DV. Only 1 mark is available, but be specific (an IV usually has at least two parts — remember the 'or not' bit).

(c) When choosing a test you probably use a flow chart. The choices you make are the reasons for deciding on the test, so outline two choices that you would make when opting for a Wilcoxon test. There is 1 mark for each.

(d) The null hypothesis is rejected when a study works and a result is significant, so you need to decide whether the result is significant or not. All the information needed is supplied. Pick out the row that you need to consider (N = ?). Then you should be able to work out the answer. You need to show your reasoning for full marks.

(e) There are 4 marks available. 1 mark is for a basic reason and further marks are for elaboration. Examples are useful when elaborating.

(f) There is 1 mark for each advantage of using a repeated measures design.

(g) There are 2 marks for giving a problem in using experiments, so remember to elaborate. Try to relate your answer to the study outlined here.

(h) There is 1 mark for noting a factor that should have been controlled. The extra mark is for elaborating and saying why that factor is important.

(i) Choose one of the main BPS ethical guidelines, briefly say what it is and what it entails to score 2 marks. For the other 2 marks, link to the study given and say how this guideline is important and why it should have been followed.

Answers to question 1

(a) There is no difference in the number of words recognised depending on whether the processing involves attending to meaning or not, and any difference is due to chance or some other variable. ✓✓

> *e* This answer gets the full 2 marks. There is mention of the 'no difference', which is what makes this a null hypothesis, and both the IV (attending to meaning or not) and the DV (recognition of words) are mentioned.

(b) Whether the participant has to process the meaning of a word or whether there is only visual processing. ✓

> *e* This answer includes both parts of the IV. If the candidate had only written 'meaning', this would not be enough for the mark.

(c) This is an independent groups design with ordinal data. ✓

> *e* This answer scores 1 mark. Although it could be argued that the data are of interval status, ordinal is not wrong. However, this is a repeated measures design, as the same participants do both conditions, so the second mark cannot be awarded. The second mark could be achieved by saying one of the following: that the same participants do both conditions; that it is a repeated measures design; that it is an experiment; that the conditions for a parametric test are not met.

(d) The null hypothesis cannot be rejected because the value of T, which is 13.5, is more than the critical value. ✓ The critical value when $N = 10$ and when the probability of the results being due to chance is equal to or less than 5% is 11. ✓ 13.5 is more than 11, so the result is not significant. ✓ The experimental hypothesis is rejected. The null is retained as it is possible that the results are due to chance or some other variable.

> *e* This is a clear answer, which easily scores all 3 marks. Note there is no mark for saying the null hypothesis is retained; it is the explanation that gets the marks.

(e) The standard deviation is used in psychology to show how the scores are spread around the mean. ✓

> *e* This answer gains 1 mark. It only defines what standard deviation is, rather than saying why it is used. Marks could be gained by giving more information, such as: standard deviation is used to see how a set of scores is spread around the mean; ✓ it is known that 68% of scores are within one standard deviation above

and below the mean; ✓ and if the SD is known then the actual scores between which 68% of the respondent scores fall are known. For example, for visual processing, 68% of the scores lie between 7.1 and 13.8 words recognised, ✓ and when meaning is processed 68% of the scores lie between 9.5 and 15.3 words recognised. It is clear that visual processing leads to fewer words being recognised. However, the differences between the two conditions are not great, and knowing the standard deviation can show this. ✓ Around 98% of scores lie within two standard deviations either side of the mean. ✓

(f) Using the same participants means that there are no participant variables. So individual differences are controlled for. There will be no difference in memory ability, for example, ✓ and no difference in age ✓ or gender.

e The overall comment about participant variables is, of course, the main point. This could have been one advantage, with another advantage given, such as less need to standardise instructions. However, as this answer focuses on the reduction of individual differences, the two factors marked are memory ability and age.

(g) An experiment tends to be unnatural and not valid. In this study, checking whether a word is written in capital letters might not represent ✓ visual processing and seeing if a word fits correctly into a sentence might not represent semantic processing (processing for meaning). These two tasks are not very natural. ✓

e This answer focuses on the actual study, as required. The first sentence sets up the answer but in itself is not clear. As soon as the answer goes on to talk about 'might not represent...' the mark is given, as this elaborates on the comment about the study not being valid. The comment that the tasks are not natural makes it clear that there is both knowledge and understanding of the disadvantage.

(h) One control is the way the words are presented to each participant. Each participant should have the same materials, ✓ and it would be better if there were a mix of visual processing and processing for meaning throughout the list, rather than all the words in one condition being presented first. ✓ If half the participants had the words that needed visual processing first and the other half had the words that needed processing for meaning first, this could lead to bias in the results.

e There are other controls, such as the use of standardised instructions, or the need to control environmental factors. This answer gives a clear factor that needs to be controlled and so gains the 2 marks. Note that the first mark is for the point made and the second mark is for elaboration.

(i) One guideline is the need for participants to know that they have the right to withdraw either themselves or their results at any time. ✓ Participants should be told about this at the start, and should be reminded about it during the study. ✓ At the end they should be asked if they agree to their results being included in the study, ✓ so that they are less likely to be left feeling uncomfortable when the study ends. ✓

This answer scores all 4 marks. Although there is no direct reference to this study, everything that is said applies. It is better to make an explicit link, such as to mention the recognition of words rather than 'results'.

This answer scores 18/22 marks.

■ ■ ■

Question 2

In psychology, some methods of data collection yield quantitative data and some give qualitative data.

(a) Define what is meant by quantitative data. (1 mark)

(b) Define what is meant by qualitative data. (1 mark)

(c) Explain how *one* named research method can give quantitative data. (3 marks)

(d) Using a different research method from the one named in (c), explain how qualitative data can be gathered. (3 marks)

(e) When collecting qualitative data, there is a risk that a researcher can be subjective. Define what is meant by subjectivity when talking about research methods. (2 marks)

(f) Discuss briefly why it is important to have objectivity when carrying out psychological research. (4 marks)

(a) Make sure you can define quantitative data correctly.

(b) Make sure you can define qualitative data correctly.

(c) Choose a method that clearly gives quantitative data. Say what the method is and show how quantitative data are gathered using that method. An example might be useful as elaboration.

(d) As in **(c)**, choose a method that clearly gives qualitative data. Say what the method is and show how qualitative data are gathered. Again, an example might be useful as elaboration.

(e) For the 2 marks, say what subjectivity means and show that you understand it. One way of elaborating would be to contrast with objectivity, or to give an example.

(f) This question is asking about bias in research and, in particular, the bias that can occur if a researcher interprets results in a subjective way. Focus on objectivity, though, and why it is important. There are 4 marks available; a useful way of elaborating is by use of an example, related to a particular method.

Answers to question 2

(a) Numerical data ✓

This is a very basic answer and not really a definition. However, quantitative data involve numbers, so the mark is given. A safer answer would say that quantitative data are measurable and are assigned numerical values.

(b) Telling a story

> Although results told in a story do involve qualitative data, this answer would not get the mark as there are many other types of qualitative data. A better answer would say that qualitative data are those where there is no numerical value but where values such as attitudes and opinions are recorded, often as a story or written comment.

(c) Experiments give quantitative data. There are careful controls and the independent variable is carefully operationalised so that it is measurable. ✓ As the intention is to measure something, the data are numerical. ✓ Not all measures are 'true' in the sense of giving interval or ratio data. However, even when categories are recorded, numbers in each category are counted. ✓

> This answer scores all 3 marks. The method is specified clearly. The first mark is given for mentioning the operationalisation of variables, as this tends to lead to quantitative data being gathered. The second mark is for saying that data are numerical. The final mark is for showing that even nominal data are quantitative.

(d) Unstructured interviews give qualitative data.

> This is not a good answer. Although the chosen method is suitable, the question asks for an explanation, so no marks are given. The answer should examine how unstructured interviews follow the thoughts of the interviewee and can be guided by the interviewee. Thus, thoughts and opinions are recorded rather than numbers, and so the data are qualitative. The main data will consist of answers to questions, such as how a person feels about environmental issues, and answers will be written down in full (or even recorded).

(e) Subjectivity refers to when the ideas, beliefs and opinions of the researcher affect what is recorded. ✓ This means that the data are subject to interpretation by the researcher, ✓ and so what one researcher records in a particular situation might vary from what another researcher records.

> This is a good answer, which scores both available marks.

(f) A study is said to be reliable if the same results are found on another occasion, or if two or more researchers record the same results on the same occasion. For this to happen, there must be objectivity. ✓ If a researcher allows his/her own opinions to affect what is recorded, then the results are likely to differ from those of another researcher. ✓ Without objectivity, the results from one situation cannot be compared reliably with the results from another situation when a study is carried out again. ✓

> This answer scores 3 marks. It is quite clear, but a bit more about bias would add the final mark. It would be useful to mention the scientific approach, which is important in some areas, and this could also gain the extra mark.

> **This answer scores 9/14 marks. Overall, the score is 27/36 marks.**

Child psychology

Question 1: Attachments and related issues

(a) Explain what is involved in the strange situation procedure. (3 marks)

(b) Evaluate the strange situation procedure as a method of studying attachment. (5 marks)

(c) Discuss the relationship between attachment type and caring style. (6 marks)

(d) Outline two criticisms of Bowlby's explanation of the mother–child relationship. (6 marks)

e **(a)** There are 3 marks available for outlining the strange situation procedure. Try to make at least three clear points about what happens.

(b) There are 5 evaluation marks available here. One point that is elaborated can score more than 1 mark, or five separate points can be made. Aim for two or three points and make sure they are elaborated and clear. Evaluation points tend to be critical, so consider what is wrong with the procedure. However, marks can also be gained by giving strengths. Examples can help when elaborating.

(c) Consider the different attachment types and then mention how they can be linked to particular caring styles, perhaps considering the sensitivity of the mother or the role of the father.

(d) Two criticisms are asked for and 6 marks are available, so assume that there are 3 marks for each criticism. 1 mark is likely to be for identifying a criticism in each case and 2 further marks for expanding on the answer.

Answers to question 1

(a) The strange situation procedure is a way of studying attachment. Ainsworth found that there are different types of attachment. It involves a researcher watching a mother and child playing, and there are different conditions. ✓

e This answer is worth 1 of the 3 marks available. The candidate mentions Ainsworth and what the procedure is for but only says that it involves different conditions and watching a mother and child playing. The conditions need to be described for the other 2 marks.

(b) A problem with the strange situation method is that cultures vary in many ways, so when it gives a result in one culture, it may give a different result in another, not for the reasons claimed but simply because of differences in the culture. ✓ For example, it was claimed that patterns of attachment in Germany are different — and the implication is that, because there are fewer securely attached children, Germans are worse at childrearing — whereas the findings may have come from a different interpretation of the procedure. ✓ In Japan, mothers don't leave their babies in the same way as in other cultures, so the procedure would not work in the same way. ✓

The main point made is that cultures vary, so findings from the procedure may be due to differences in culture. This is one of the main points of the procedure — that it finds that there are differences in attachment types in different cultures. However, the point made here is that there may be cultural differences in reactions to the procedure, not in attachment types. This is a difficult point to make and is not well made here, but 1 mark is given for the main point and 2 further marks for the two examples (Germany and Japan). The other 2 marks could have come from criticising the method, and saying it leads to an unnatural situation, or by pointing out that the procedure does not take the temperament of the child into account. Marks can be gained by giving positive points about the procedure (e.g. that it allows something as complicated as attachment to be measured).

(c) There are generally thought to be three main attachment types. Ainsworth did a lot of studies in this area. In one study she compared Ugandan mothers with mothers in Baltimore in the USA. She found similar attachment types in both cases. ✓ She found that children who were not really attached tended to have mothers who were not around as much as mothers who had securely attached children. ✓ She thought that responsive mothers (those who were around a lot) had more securely attached children, and this suggests that attachment type links to caring style. ✓ Fathers seem to have a different caring style — they play with their children more ✓ — and yet children can be just as attached to the father as to the mother. So it is not likely that one caring style (being responsive) leads to strong attachments — different relationships seem to yield strong attachments. ✓ There can even be multiple attachments, and it seems likely that these different attachment figures are likely to give different caring styles. ✓

This answer scores all 6 marks. There is a good discussion about the links between attachments and caring style. First, the comparison of two cultures and finding similar attachment types is given a mark, as it sets up the comment that securely attached children have responsive mothers. A third mark is given for concluding that attachment type might come from caring style. The point about fathers gets a mark, as does the conclusion that different caring styles can still lead to strong attachments. A final mark is given for the comment about multiple attachments.

(d) One problem with Bowlby's explanation about mother–child relationships is that he based his idea quite firmly on one of his own studies, the study of juvenile thieves, and yet there are criticisms of that study. ✓ One criticism is that the participants had been in an institution as well as having been deprived of their mothers. ✓ Rutter suggests that those in an institution are not stimulated as much, and it is the lack of stimulation rather than the lack of a mother that gives the problems. ✓

Another problem is that he fails to take into account that there can be multiple attachments. ✓ So being maternally deprived might not be as problematic as Bowlby suggested and monotropy does not exist ✓ — the child does not have just a single attachment figure. ✓

This answer scores all 6 marks. 2 marks are for identifying the two problems. Rutter's point about lack of stimulation is well made and a conclusion quite clearly drawn, so 2 elaboration marks are given. The criticism that monotropy does not exist is also quite well elaborated, although perhaps the last mark is rather generous. A little more (e.g. an example of multiple attachments by mentioning siblings and fathers) would have made sure of that last mark.

■ ■ ■

Question 2: Deprivation, privation, institutional care, divorce and related areas

(a) Define deprivation. (1 mark)

(b) Define privation. (1 mark)

(c) Describe *one* study into the effects of privation. (4 marks)

(d) Discuss the extent to which the effects of privation are reversible. (6 marks)

(e) Describe *one* study into the effects of institutional care on children. (5 marks)

(f) Identify *two* possible effects of parental separation or divorce on children. (4 marks)

(g) What difficulties have psychologists encountered in investigating the effects of parental separation or divorce on children? (6 marks)

(a) 1 mark is available for saying what the term means. An example alone is not enough as a definition but it may help if you are not sure that you have expressed yourself clearly.

(b) 1 mark is available for saying what the term means. As before, an example alone is not likely to be enough.

(c) This is a standard question asking for description of a study of your choice. There will be a mark for giving the aim of the study (thereby identifying it) and marks for a description of the method, the results and conclusions. Remember that just outlining the method or describing the results will not get full marks. Be ready for this question in any of the areas you have studied. You could prepare an answer. Focus on studies of privation (no bond formed), not deprivation (separation from caregiver).

(d) 6 marks are available for a clear discussion. You might choose to make two points in some depth or you might decide to give several points. Don't describe the effects of privation — make sure that each point is about whether the effects can be reversed or not.

(e) The same advice applies as for **(c)**.

(f) This question simply asks for identification (AO1 knowledge and understanding). As there are 4 marks available, don't just give one word of identification for each effect. Say enough to earn 2 marks in each case.

(g) 6 marks are available, so in theory you could give six difficulties. However, a better way of answering would be to choose two or three difficulties and outline them clearly. Examples might be useful. Remember to focus on problems in investigating. This question is really about methodology and ethics.

Answers to question 2

(a) Deprivation means that a child has had some form of attachment with a caregiver and then that attachment has been broken by separation in some way. So the child is deprived of the attachment figure. ✓

e This scores the mark. It is clear that the candidate knows what deprivation means.

(b) Privation is not like deprivation.

e This answer does not get the mark, although the statement is true. More is needed, such as saying that in the case of privation no attachment is formed in the first place, so the child is privated of any form of attachment.

(c) Koluchova studied the effects of privation in twin boys. The boys had had a little care early on in their lives, although it is not known what this was like. They were found at the age of about 6 and were very behind in measures of development such as language and IQ. The aim of the study was to see what the effects of privation were — could the effects be reversed? ✓ The twins were fostered with great care and their IQ was measured quite frequently. ✓ Their IQ became normal and they seemed to overcome the effects of the early privation. ✓ It was concluded that extra special care could reverse the effects of privation. ✓

e The full 4 marks are awarded. 1 mark is for the aim — to see if the effects of privation could be reversed; 1 mark is for the method — saying that their IQ was measured frequently and that they were fostered with extra care; 1 mark is for the result — that their IQ became normal; and a further mark is for the conclusion — that good quality care can reverse the effects of privation. This is a case study and it is hard to give marks in the same way as for an experiment. The method and results, for example, are not so clearly defined. Therefore, case studies tend to be marked a little differently.

(d) Koluchova showed in her study of twins who were privated early in their lives that the effects of privation are reversible. ✓ When they were found, the twins had very low IQ scores and could not walk or use language normally for their age. But they were fostered and later developed enough to have normal IQ and normal development. ✓ However, the study of Genie shows that the effects of privation are not reversible. ✓ Genie was looked after by psychologists from the age of about 13 and made a small amount of progress but did not become 'normal'. ✓

e This answer scores 4 of the 6 marks available. The candidate clearly knows about the Koluchova study, which shows that the effects are reversible, and the Genie study, which shows that they are not. Marks are given for each piece of research and each of the conclusions. In each case, the 2 marks are for the information and for elaboration, rather than one for the study and one for the point. For the extra 2 marks, the candidate could have made some evaluation points, for example pointing out that the twins had each other, so might not have been truly privated, and Genie could have had a problem with development from the start.

(e) One study is that of Skeels and Dye (1939). At the age of 2, some children from an orphanage were sent to a home for retarded women. ✓ Other children stayed at the orphanage. The IQs of all the children were measured before the two groups were split. ✓ Those who went to the home were 'mothered' by the women and stimulated by them. When the children were just over 3 years old their IQs were measured again. Those who had stayed at the orphanage had lower IQ scores than those who had had some stimulation. ✓ It was concluded that stimulation of any kind helps intellectual development, whereas staying in an institution does not. ✓

> *e* This answer is awarded 4 of the 5 marks. No aim is stated and the identification of the study is not enough. Giving the aim would have gained a mark. There are 2 clear method marks. There is 1 mark for the main result — that those who were stimulated had a higher IQ afterwards — and 1 mark for the conclusion — that stimulation helps intellectual development. Further marks would have been awarded for more about the conclusion or the results.

(f) One possible effect of separation or divorce is that if the child is under 2 years old, separation from the mother can lead to distress ✓ and, according to some studies, even juvenile delinquency when the child is older. ✓ Another possible effect is that there is no model relationship for a child, ✓ so later in life that child will find it difficult to form relationships. ✓

> *e* This answer scores all 4 marks. There are two effects (possible juvenile delinquency and problems forming relationships when older) and in both cases the points are elaborated quite clearly for the extra 2 marks.

(g) One problem is when parents don't want to be interviewed or don't want their child to be interviewed. ✓ Another problem is that it is hard to take into account that different children have different temperaments in any case, so what might affect one child one way might affect another child in a different way. ✓ A child who is anxious might react differently from a child who is angry. ✓

> *e* This answer scores 3 marks out of the 6 available. The first problem is fine but needs elaborating. It would be useful to say why they might not want to be interviewed, or why ethical issues would then mean that data cannot be gathered. The second problem is elaborated enough for a second mark. Another mark could be gained by saying why it is hard to take into account different temperaments.

■ ■ ■

Question 3: Play, friendships and popularity

(a) Outline *one* type of children's play. (2 marks)

(b) Compare and contrast *two* theories of play. (12 marks)

(c) Outline *one* factor that can affect the popularity of a particular child. (3 marks)

(d) Give *two* criticisms of the validity of research into childhood popularity. (6 marks)

(e) Discuss cultural differences in peer relationships. (12 marks)

(a) 2 marks are available, 1 mark for the type of play and a further mark for saying something about it. An example might help to elaborate.

(b) This is an essay question. You will be told on the front of the paper which are the essay questions. Note that essay questions, when they occur, are always the last question of a topic and are worth 12–18 marks. Of the 12 marks available here, 2 are for clarity and communication and 2 are for balance and breadth. This leaves 4 AO1 marks and 4 AO2 marks. So there are likely to be 2 marks for each theory of play and 4 marks for anything that says how they are similar or different.

(c) There is likely to be 1 mark for the factor and 2 for information about it.

(d) There is likely to be 1 mark for each criticism and 2 more marks in each case for saying clearly what the criticism is and giving evidence. This question is about method and whether there is validity or not, so you must discuss how such research might lack validity.

(e) This is another essay question, so look at the comments for part **(b)**. The AO1 marks are for giving cultural differences and the AO2 marks are for giving evaluative points. The evaluative points can be research evidence for the AO1 points made, or they could be other points, such as criticisms of methods used.

Answers to question 3

(a) Cooperative play ✓ is where children play together and share toys. ✓

This answer scores both marks as the type of play is clearly identified.

(b) Two theories of play are the cognitive–developmental approach and the psychodynamic approach. Cognitive-developmental theorists suggest that play has a role in intellectual development and that it contributes to a child's cognitive development. ✓ (AO1) For example, Piaget's mastery stage of play is where children begin to gain mastery over their environment. ✓ (AO1) However, the psychodynamic approach suggests that, although play does help children to gain mastery over their environment, it is gaining mastery over negative events, rather than growing cognitively in a positive manner. ✓ (AO2) The psychodynamic approach would say that play helps a child to work through negative emotions so that they no longer affect the child in a negative way. ✓ (AO1) For example, children, through play, can act out situations between themselves and their parents, perhaps using dolls. ✓ (AO1, max) Cognitive–developmental theorists don't see play as helping a child to gain power over a situation in the same way. Play helps the child to develop, cognitively and socially. ✓ (AO2)

Vygotsky emphasised the importance of social interaction to cognitive development. Cognitive–developmental theorists suggest that play helps a child to develop intellectually and to build up to formal reasoning. However, the psychodynamic viewpoint focuses on helping the child emotionally by working through problematic situations. The idea of focusing on emotions seems more likely, as it seems clear that there is more to play than just learning about thinking — children do

get emotional when playing, and they do use toys to represent issues in their lives. ✓ (AO2) Another difference between the cognitive–developmental and the psychodynamic theories of play is that the psychodynamic approach has a practical application and has developed a therapy, whereas the cognitive–developmental approach has not. ✓ (AO2)

e This answer gains full marks. There are four clear AO1 points and 4 marks available. The two theories are outlined well, for 2 marks each. There are four AO2 points too. Here, the candidate indicates that both theories are about mastery over the environment, but one is about mastery in a cognitive sense and one is about mastery in an emotional sense. This point is elaborated later for another mark, when it is said that it seems more likely that play has a role in developing emotions as well as thinking. It is an elaboration on the same point to say that the two approaches talk about power over the situation in different ways, so overall this one main point is awarded 3 AO2 marks. Another AO2 mark is gained for saying that one theory has a practical application and the other does not. This is not expanded upon but, given what has already been said, it is clear what is meant. There is a good balanced argument, so both balance/breadth marks are given. There is good use of terminology, and the written communication is fine, so both clarity/communication marks are given too.

(c) The popularity of a particular child can come from his/her social skills. ✓ Those with appropriate social skills (e.g. good communication skills) tend to be more popular. Good social skills may come from a positive relationship with their parents. ✓

e This answer scores 2 marks out of 3. A reference to some research would help to get the other mark, or some elaboration of good communication skills (e.g. it makes other children feel comfortable or it makes interactions easier).

(d) Validity of research into popularity can be questioned because popularity is determined culturally and there are cultural differences in what is popular. ✓ Good communication skills might be valued in Western culture but in China children who are shy can still be popular. ✓ So findings from research in one culture should not be generalised to all cultures; research in one culture is valid only in that culture. ✓ Another problem regarding validity is that popularity can change from day to day. A child who is popular for one period of time is not necessarily always popular, or popular with all other children. ✓ Thus a researcher might observe a particular child and patterns of popularity on one day but on a different occasion the factors that predict popularity may be different, ✓ so what is being measured can change, which brings into question the validity of the research. ✓

e This answer scores all 6 marks. It focuses on two criticisms, and both relate to validity. Another related point would be that popularity is a difficult concept to measure, so it is hard to be sure that any measure chosen is valid.

(e) What is popular in one culture is not necessarily popular in another. For example, in China shy children are not rejected because of their shyness, whereas in Western cultures shy children are less likely to be popular. ✓ **(AO1)**

When interacting with peers, popularity is an important feature, so it seems that peer relationships are likely to vary from culture to culture. ✓ **(AO1)** One problem with research is that it is often carried out mainly in one culture, and the findings are generalised to all cultures. With many features of human interactions, there are cultural differences; peer relationships are likely to show cultural differences too. So what is found in one culture may not necessarily apply to another culture and care should be taken with findings. ✓ **(AO2)**

One way in which cultural differences have been measured is to say that a culture is predominantly collectivist or individualist. This means that people either work together for the good of the culture (collectivist) or work for themselves for their own goals (individualist). ✓ **(AO1)** It has been found that children in these different types of culture show different peer relationships. As would be expected, children in a collectivist culture, such as a kibbutz in Israel, tend to cooperate with one another to achieve goals and when playing. ✓ **(AO1, max)** Children in an individualist culture, as Western cultures tend to be, are more likely to compete than to cooperate, as they are encouraged towards individual achievement.

There are many complex factors involved when looking at friendships and peer relationships, so it is not an easy area to study, and validity of research is doubtful given that the variables are difficult to isolate and measure. ✓ **(AO2)** Studies have found that the socialisation patterns of a culture do tend to predict friendship patterns, so it seems that nurture, not nature, leads to type of friendship, and if studies support one another, then this is evidence. ✓ **(AO2)**

e All 4 AO1 marks are awarded. There is a mark for the knowledge that in China shyness does not lead to unpopularity and a mark for elaborating by drawing the conclusion about culture and popularity. The other AO1 marks are for the point about the two different types of culture and the elaboration using the example of kibbutzim in Israel. Of the 4 AO2 marks available, 3 are awarded. 1 mark is for commenting that findings from studies in one culture should not be generalised to other cultures, 1 mark is for saying that variables are hard to measure and the final AO2 mark is for saying that studies do support one another, so this is evidence. If this latter point were clearer, another AO2 mark could have been gained. The arguments are good and clear, and the answer is both broad and balanced, so both balance/breadth marks are gained. Terminology is good too, and communication is clear, so both clarity/communication marks are gained. This answer scores 11 out of 12 available marks.

Environmental psychology

Question 1: Personal space and territoriality

(a) What is meant by territoriality? (2 marks)

(b) Outline *two* consequences of the invasion of personal space. (4 marks)

(c) Outline *one* advantage and one disadvantage of applying the concept of territoriality to human behaviour. (6 marks)

(d) Discuss *two* functions of territoriality. (12 marks)

(e) Outline *one* example of poor architectural design. (3 marks)

(f) A local authority is planning to regenerate a run-down housing estate. Based on psychological research, explain what advice you would give to the local authority. (5 marks)

e **(a)** You need to say what territoriality is and expand on it, perhaps by giving an example.

(b) There are 4 marks available, 2 for each consequence. For 1 mark say what each consequence is and for the other mark say more about it.

(c) When there are two requirements, such as outline an advantage and a disadvantage, assume that the marks are equally divided. In this case, there would be 3 marks for the advantage and 3 for the disadvantage. Expect there to be 1 mark each for the actual advantage and disadvantage and then 2 further marks in each case for elaboration.

(d) This is an essay question. The essay question is always the last question within each application, and is worth 12–18 marks. Of the 12 marks available here, 2 are for balance and breadth, and 2 are for quality of written communication, including use of terminology. This leaves, 4 AO1 marks and 4 AO2 marks. As two functions are asked for, there are 2 AO1 marks and 2 AO2 marks for each function.

(e) 3 marks are available. 1 mark is likely to be for the example itself and the other 2 marks are for describing it.

(f) All your advice must be based on psychological research. A good way of answering this question is to give two or three pieces of advice and briefly outline the relevant research.

Answers to question 1

(a) Territoriality refers to people's feelings that they own a certain area and they try to mark their territory to maintain that ownership or feeling of ownership. ✓

e This is not quite enough for 2 marks. An example would have helped, such as talking about wasteland outside people's houses which can be maintained by them and be seen as their territory.

(b) Invading someone's personal space can lead to aggression. ✓ Personal space varies according to the relationship two people have but, whatever the space, we protect it (mentally) and invading it can lead to fights and aggressive reactions. ✓ Another consequence of invading someone's space is that we are less helpful when our space is invaded. ✓ Studies show that we help others more often when our personal space is protected, perhaps because we feel more secure and less aggressive. ✓

e This answer gains all 4 marks. Two consequences are given and examples and/or elaboration help to explain them.

(c) Evidence shows that humans do mark territory and the concept of territoriality helps to explain human behaviour, which is an advantage. For example, students might leave a bag on their desk to mark it as their own, ✓ and people mark out their territory on the beach. ✓ People build boundary fences around their property and argue over such areas. ✓ A disadvantage is that this is only one explanation ✓ and people might build a fence to protect their children or their property rather than to mark their territory. ✓ It is quite a narrow view and only looks at one fairly biological explanation, whereas there are many cultural and social factors that can explain such behaviour. ✓

e This answer scores all 6 marks. The mark for the advantage is given here after one example — it is useful to give an example as evidence when a question asks about links to human behaviour. The other examples get the other marks as there is elaboration. 3 marks are only just given as the point relies a little too much on common sense and there is not enough psychology. The disadvantage is quite well outlined and again examples are given to good effect.

(d) Territory serves the function of allowing privacy. ✓ (AO1) Privacy concerns how much people want to make themselves available to others. There is desired privacy, which is what we want to achieve, and achieved privacy, which is what we actually get. ✓ (AO1) Sometimes we cannot maintain desired privacy. Territory helps as we can defend territory and lay down markers, which deter others from coming too close, and in this way privacy can be maintained. Territory is also useful to organise people into groups. ✓ (AO1) Gangs can mark their territory and violence can be prevented if they do not enter into each other's territory. ✓ (AO1) Neighbourhoods can be organised using territory markers and this can give people a sense of belonging.

e There are 2 AO1 marks for each function and these are easily gained here as the two functions are clear and both are elaborated upon. However, there are no evaluation points, so no AO2 marks are gained. The functions are outlined well, with examples, so 2 balance/breadth marks are given. There is good use of terminology and good communication too, so 2 clarity/communication marks are given. This answer scores 8 out of 12 marks. AO2 points could include criticisms of studies — for example, studies tend to take place in specific cultures and yet concepts such as personal space can vary between cultures. So perhaps findings from studies should not be generalised to all cultures, as is the case in the answer given here. Similarly, there are other factors, not just territory, involved in maintaining privacy as well as in delineating social groups.

(e) One example is the Pruitt–Igoe estate where there were many high-rise flats. Numerous problems arose, which seemed to be because of the design. ✓ The community areas were not convenient and the residents did not use them. The areas were just too far away. ✓ There was a lot of crime and vandalism. The flats were demolished quite soon after they were built. ✓

e **3 marks are awarded as the example is quite well outlined.**

(f) Newman explained that a large part of satisfactory communal living has to do with ownership. If people feel they own the surrounding areas and take responsibility for them, the territory is better looked after and so there are fewer problems. ✓ A local authority needs to make sure that there is not much land or not many areas that are seen as not belonging to anyone or some group. ✓ Flats that are only three storeys high, with six in a block, are best, because the residents then see any communal areas as jointly owned, and this means they are watched over. ✓ Tower blocks can mean nobody takes ownership of, for example, stairs, and so problems can arise. So build only small blocks. ✓ Areas of open land should be fenced off and allocated to a group of residents for their use. ✓

e **The maximum 5 marks are awarded. The answer gives examples and advice. The examples and theory are credited as they reinforce or explain the advice.**

■ ■ ■

Question 2: Environmental stress and crowding

(a) Outline what is meant by environmental stress. (3 marks)

(b) Describe *one* study of the effects of environmental stress. (5 marks)

(c) Give *two* criticisms of the study you have just described. (6 marks)

(d) Discuss strategies for coping with environmental stress. (12 marks)

(e) Discuss practical and ethical issues raised by research into crowding in humans and/or animals. (8 marks)

(f) Discuss the effects of high-density living on humans. (12 marks)

e **(a)** There are 3 marks available, so a simple definition is not enough. Examples are useful when outlining or describing but they must always be linked clearly to the answer.

(b) When describing a study, identify its aim. Then focus on method, results and conclusions. There is a maximum of 2 marks for each of these areas, so you will not get full marks if you focus on one of them.

(c) When two questions are linked in this way, make sure you talk about the study you have just described. There are 6 marks available, so assume there are 3 marks for each criticism. 1 mark is likely to be for the criticism itself and 2 marks in each case for elaborating and making the point clear.

(d) This is an essay question. See the comment relating to Question 1(d).

(e) 8 marks are available. It is unlikely that there are 4 marks for talking about practical issues and 4 marks for ethical issues. There might, however, be a maximum 6 marks if only ethical or practical issues are given. When looking at animal studies, it is hard to separate practical and ethical issues, so marks are likely to be given according to points made rather than whether they are practical or ethical.

(f) This is an essay for 12 marks. Any points showing knowledge and understanding about high-density living and humans and anything you say to elaborate upon such points will be awarded marks. There are 4 AO1 marks, so you could make two clear points and then elaborate, or you could make four clear points, or any combination. Then you need to score 4 AO2 marks. These could be gained by criticising research, for example looking at the methods or ethics. You could also look at contradicting evidence if, for example, findings of studies vary. There might be some general points you could make, such as if studies are done in a particular culture you could discuss whether the findings can be generalised to another culture.

Answers to question 2

(a) Stress occurs when people think their resources are insufficient to cope with the demands of a situation. Environmental stress is when the situation giving stress comes from the environment. ✓ Environmental stressors are factors in the background and in our environment that lead to stress, such as noise. ✓ When we can cope with such stressors, we may not experience environmental stress but when environmental factors cannot be coped with, then we might experience stress. ✓

e This answer scores all 3 marks. The basic idea of stress is clearly outlined and the example of environmental stress also gains a mark. There is a further mark for restating the issue to make it clearer.

(b) Glass and Singer (1972) carried out a study looking at the effect of noise on performance. ✓ There was loud noise, soft noise, regular noise and random noise, so there were four conditions. ✓ The noise took place while participants were carrying out cognitive tasks. ✓ Some participants were able to control the noise. Performance was worst when the participants had loud noise that was unpredictable and uncontrollable. ✓ It was concluded that this was an environmental after-effect. ✓

e Full marks are achieved here. The aim is clear and there are 2 clear method marks. There are also 2 marks for results.

(c) This was an experiment, so the conditions were not natural. The tasks were not real ones and the participants knew that a study was taking place. So it could be said that the results are not valid. ✓ However, we are subject to various types of noise and we do carry out unfamiliar cognitive tasks sometimes, so the findings are of interest, particularly in those situations. ✓ Other studies have shown that being able to control a stressor can mean that less stress is experienced, so the findings are backed by others. ✓ It could be that this study was unethical, as the participants were said to have become frustrated.

e The point about lack of validity is quite well made and scores 2 marks. The point about other studies could do with some evidence but there is just enough for 1 mark. Giving another study would have been useful though and could have gained another mark. The point about this study being unethical is also quite clear and would get a mark, but is a third criticism and only two were asked for.

(d) Environmental stress can be coped with in the same way as other types of stress, using problem-focused or emotion-focused strategies, or defence mechanisms. ✓ (AO1) Problem-focusing could entail removing the source of stress ✓ (AO1) or gaining more control over it. ✓ (AO1) Glass and Singer found that uncontrollable noise increased stress, so if noise is predictable or controllable it might be less stressful. ✓ (AO2) Defence mechanisms might not be useful as it is unlikely that a loud noise can be ignored. ✓ (AO2) Practical coping mechanisms are usually best, as removing the stressor is a good way to cope with stress. ✓ (AO2) Emotion-focusing can mean changing the way we think about a stressor ✓ (AO1) and perhaps understanding it is one way of doing this. If we know why we are stressed — for example, due to heat — then we may cope with it better. ✓ (AO2)

e Full marks are achieved here. Problem-focusing is outlined in two ways, for 2 AO1 marks. Mentioning three ways of coping in the first sentence gets an AO1 mark too. The final AO1 mark is for outlining what emotion-focusing can mean. The evidence from the Glass and Singer study is given an AO2 mark as evidence is used to back the point, and there is an AO2 mark for saying that practical ways are best. There is also an AO2 mark for saying that denial might not work, and one for saying that understanding might help. There is plenty of information here, with depth and breadth, so 2 balance/breadth marks are given. 2 clarity/communication marks are awarded for good communication and use of appropriate terms.

(e) One practical issue when researching crowding in humans is that it is hard to gather data. ✓ When crowds form it is not easy to notice everything about the situation. ✓ Similarly, there might be many factors affecting the crowd behaviour, such as cultural factors and environmental factors like noise and heat. ✓ So it is hard to gather the necessary information, since operationalising variables is difficult. ✓ Ethical problems are also important. We could not deliberately subject people to uncomfortable crowded conditions to see their reactions. For one thing, these reactions are likely to be aggressive — making people aggressive is not ethical. ✓ It would be hard to give the right to withdraw too, as in a crowded situation it is hard to do so. ✓ We could not gain informed consent either, as knowing what was being done might affect behaviour. ✓ This is both a practical and an ethical problem. Calhoun studied rats by deliberately putting them into crowded conditions and they became aggressive and cannibalistic. This could be seen as unethical. ✓

e All 8 marks are awarded here as several points are made, both practical and ethical issues are addressed, and the answer focuses on humans and animals.

(f) In general, humans do not respond well to high-density living. People in high-density conditions are more anxious than those in less crowded conditions, ✓ (AO1) but there are other factors, too. For example, those with control over the situation are less stressed than those who have no control, ✓ (AO1) so it is not just the high-density conditions that cause the stress. ✓ (AO2) High-density conditions mean that there are a lot of people to a small area, ✓ (AO1) which is the same as crowding, although crowding tends to imply a negative emotion whereas high-density living may not. ✓ (AO2). The problem is density, that is, when there are a lot of people in a small space. So it is not just high-rise buildings, as the apartments might be quite spacious, but the actual size of the homes and how many people live there. ✓ (AO2) High-density living can affect cognitive development and children can be less sociable. ✓ (AO1) However, studies can be experimental so they do not necessarily yield valid results. Some conclusions about crowding come from animal studies, so the findings may not be applicable to humans. ✓ (AO2)

e Full marks are awarded for this answer. It is well balanced and easily deserves the 2 balance/breadth marks. The 2 clarity/communication marks are given too.

■ ■ ■

Question 3: Changing behaviour to save the environment

(a) What explanations have psychologists put forward for the idea that human behaviour is often not environmentally friendly with regard to recycling? (7 marks)

(b) Assess the effectiveness of rewards and punishments in encouraging environmentally responsible behaviour. (4 marks)

(c) How might ways of changing attitudes by use of promotional literature affect recycling behaviour? (8 marks)

e **(a)** This question is asking you to describe the arguments about recycling behaviour, in particular focusing on why we don't recycle. Focus on giving the arguments and outlining various pieces of research or findings that show that we are not environmentally friendly in our behaviour.

(b) There are 4 marks available here. You need to discuss how effective rewards and punishments are, perhaps by considering alternative methods and contrasting them, or by looking at studies and giving their findings.

(c) Here you can talk about what promotional literature is, give examples of how it has changed behaviour and, if appropriate, in what circumstances it does not work.

Answers to question 3

(a) Human behaviour is often not environmentally friendly when it comes to recycling. This is because a resource is desired and there is a dilemma between having the desired resource and knowing that it will run out, so working to preserve it. ✓

When a situation gets worse, people do become more environmentally friendly, perhaps because they realise more clearly that the resource will run out if they don't. ✓ Then again, when the resource gets even more scarce, there might be less environmentally friendly behaviour as people rush to get what they can for themselves. One reason psychologists use is conformity — if more people were environmentally friendly we would conform, but when people are not, then we tend not to act in this 'friendly' way. ✓

e This answer focuses on the question to an extent and 3 marks are given out of the 7 available. However, it would benefit from some studies or evidence. Gifford (1997) points out that we could try to encourage environmentally friendly behaviour by making it worth people's while to stop plundering resources, but that we could not afford this in all cases. So one psychological reason is simply that unfriendly behaviour is rewarded. Detail like this would gain the extra marks.

(b) Evidence is mixed because studies do not always find the same results. One study showed that increasing rewards for individuals was more effective than increasing the reward for the whole group, and this suggests that selfish behaviour is involved. ✓ However, another study found that when the winnings of the group were to be divided at the end, raising the reward for the whole group helped. ✓ Simulations are involved and this could be the problem, as the rules tend to be very complex and this is not likely to reflect real life. ✓ Overall it seems that evidence shows rewards with punishments to be the best option. On the one hand, rewards are given, such as social acceptability; on the other hand, there are punishments such as fines to encourage the behaviour. ✓ Neither rewards nor punishments on their own seem to be as good as both together.

e There is some good evaluation here, looking at evidence and at the role of rewards and punishments together, so the 4 marks are easily achieved.

(c) Changing attitudes is not an easy thing to do, but advertising and promotional literature can help. The Yale model of persuasive communication suggests that there is importance in who the messenger is and who is listening, as well as what the actual message is. ✓ The message must be attended to, understood and accepted before attitudes will change. In addition, the message must be remembered. ✓ So if recycling behaviour is to be changed, the person giving the message must be clear and well respected, ✓ the message must be phrased in an understandable way, ✓ people must be in a position where they can attend to the message and not be distracted, ✓ and reminders must be organised.

e 5 marks are awarded. The model is quite well outlined and it is applied well with suggestions for changing behaviour. An example for the last point, to show how reminders might work, would have scored further marks. Evidence for different aspects of the model could also have been given, such as details about the speaker (e.g. being similar to the audience).

Health psychology

Question 1: Health and substance abuse

(a) Define addiction. (1 mark)

(b) Define withdrawal. (1 mark)

(c) How useful is learning theory as an explanation of addiction? (8 marks)

(d) Describe the psychological effects of *one* addictive drug you have studied. (4 marks)

(e) Discuss how people are affected psychologically by abstinence after long-term drug use. (6 marks)

(f) Describe cognitive factors of addiction. (3 marks)

(a) There is 1 mark for saying what addiction is. Make sure that you can define words that appear in the specification.

(b) As for part **(a)**, this answer needs a simple definition but, if in doubt, give an example, to make sure you show knowledge with understanding.

(c) This question is asking you to evaluate learning theory and the way it explains addiction. You can do this by giving general criticisms of learning theory. You could also give alternative explanations of addiction but you will not get full marks if you just do this.

(d) Choose one drug and make sure it is identifiable. Explain how it works in terms of psychology. Psychological effects tend to be to do with cognition (thinking) or feeling, rather than biological factors. There are 4 marks available, so two effects that are explained well would be one way of getting full marks.

(e) Discuss good and bad psychological effects of abstinence. You could achieve all 6 marks by making six clear points, or you could give two or three points and expand upon them.

(f) Cognitive factors are psychological ones. Focus on any thoughts that are linked to addiction to drugs. These can involve self-esteem, for example, or reasons that people give for taking drugs. There are 3 marks available; these can be gained by giving three separate factors or by expanding upon two.

Answers to question 1

(a) Addiction refers to when someone has to keep taking a drug.

This is not wrong but it is what anyone could say. Addiction is when someone is either psychologically or physiologically dependent on a drug, or both. This means that they rely on it to feel good (psychological dependence) or they need it for the normal functioning of their body (physiological dependence). This answer might get a mark but don't take a chance — give a clear definition.

(b) Withdrawal is the term used to refer to symptoms that occur when people stop taking a drug after they have become addicted to it. ✓

This answer is clear enough, for 1 mark.

(c) Although there are perhaps pleasurable consequences from drug taking, this is not always the case. For example, smoking may not be a pleasurable experience at first. ✓ So operant conditioning may not be a good explanation. Drugs that give pleasure at one stage sometimes do not give a pleasurable experience later but people are still addicted to them. ✓ Looking at a heroin addict and considering the social problems this can bring, it does not seem that pleasure is the reason for using the drug. ✓ Social learning theory, though, is quite a good explanation. For example, it has been shown that if parents smoke it is more likely that their children will smoke. ✓ Then again, not all children of parents who smoke are smokers themselves. ✓ Also, if children see that smoking affects their parents' health, this does not mean that the children don't smoke, although modelling might predict that this would happen. ✓

e Six clear points are made, for 6 marks. For the extra marks, you could say that classical conditioning is a useful way of treating addiction rather than an explanation of how addiction occurs, and expand on this. In addition, more specific examples of drugs could be used — for example, how alcohol is often taken in social situations, which would fit both social learning and operant conditioning explanations.

(d) Alcohol has psychological effects in that it leads to a loss of inhibitions in social situations and this can mean that people behave in a way they would not usually do. ✓ At first, alcohol may lead to feelings of happiness and being more liberated in company — a psychological effect. ✓ However, it is likely to lead to poor reasoning ability and poor memory, ✓ both of which can be called psychological effects. If people are less inhibited when they have drunk alcohol, they might repeat the behaviour because of the effect — another psychological effect of alcohol. ✓

e This answer scores all 4 marks. The first mark is for talking about feeling less inhibited and the second is for saying that a person can feel happier. A third mark is given for the mention of cognitive effects (poor reasoning ability and poor memory). The final mark is for talking about the law of effect.

(e) Abstaining from a drug can have psychological consequences. Withdrawal symptoms may be severe, for example headaches and feelings of nausea. There may be psychological symptoms, such as feeling irritable and anxious. ✓ Cravings may also be experienced. Psychological dependence on a drug means that the person relies on it to feel good, ✓ so abstaining means that other measures have to be taken to feel good, or at least that this reliance is broken. ✓ Therapy can help — for example, with the use of classical conditioning techniques or counselling. ✓

e This answer receives 4 of the 6 available marks. Examples would add more marks — for example, discussing alcohol and giving it up. Classical conditioning treatments such as aversion therapy can work up to a point, and the use of drugs such as Antabuse may help, but in a social situation where drink was used to help social interaction, there may be associations that make abstinence difficult.

(f) Cognitive factors include attitudes to health and can relate to the health belief model. For example, if young people are surveyed to see why they smoke, it seems their reasons include attitudes to smoking and whether they think their health will be at risk. ✓ If they don't think they are at risk and they don't have a negative attitude to smoking, they are likely to continue. ✓ The same can be said for other drugs such as Ecstasy. There is a tendency to think that any problems won't happen to them. ✓ These are cognitive factors.

> This answer scores all 3 marks. One point is about smokers thinking it won't happen to them, one point is about the level of risk, and the third mark is for elaboration, mentioning smoking and Ecstasy.

■ ■ ■

Question 2: Stress

(a) Explain what is meant by stress. (2 marks)

(b) Describe the physiological response to stress. (4 marks)

(c) Discuss emotion-focused strategies for coping with stress. (12 marks)

(d) How effective are coping strategies for managing stress? (6 marks)

(e) Choose *two* resources and discuss how important they are in coping with stress. (6 marks)

> **(a)** The 2 marks here are for defining stress and expanding on your answer, perhaps by giving a relevant example.
>
> **(b)** All 4 marks are for saying what the biological/physiological response to stress is, so focus on that.
>
> **(c)** This is a 12-mark essay question. There will be 2 balance/breadth marks available for a balanced answer that covers quite a few points and 2 clarity/communication marks available for use of relevant terminology and good quality written communication. This leaves 4 AO1 marks and 4 AO2 marks. All points should be about emotion-focused strategies. For example, 1 mark could be for defining this. AO2 marks can be gained by comparing emotion-focused and problem-focused strategies, but make sure all your points have something to do with emotion-focusing.
>
> **(d)** All 6 marks are about the effectiveness of coping strategies and for this answer you can give emotion-focusing, problem-focusing and defence mechanisms in any combination. You could say that one is better than another in general, or that in certain situations one is not as good. You could say that one strategy suits a certain type of person better than another. There are no marks for describing coping strategies.
>
> **(e)** You need to identify two resources for coping with stress, for 1 mark each. The other 2 marks in each case are for explaining what the resource is and how it is used in coping. Examples can help to illustrate these points.

Answers to question 2

(a) Stress occurs when the demands of a situation go beyond the resources a person has for coping. ✓ This can vary from person to person as individuals have different resources and may perceive the demands of a situation differently. ✓

e **2 marks are achieved here. The first sentence is clear and the second elaborates sufficiently.**

(b) Stress involves internal and external factors. There are events in our lives that can cause stress; stress occurs when we are not coping with those events, or think we cannot cope.

e **This answer does not focus on physiological factors at all, so no marks are given. The sympathetic part of the nervous system activates various physiological factors, such as increased blood flow and heart rate, as well as increasing breathing rate and slowing digestion. These factors are in preparation for fight or flight. There is secretion of corticosteroids and an increase in protein and fat mobilisation. The parasympathetic part of the autonomic nervous system has a role in calming and taking the system back to a normal state, without the alarm reaction. This is the sort of detail needed for the 4 marks.**

(c) One emotion-focused strategy for coping is counselling, where a helping relationship is provided. When there is a close support network, less stress is suffered. ✓ **(AO1)** Having social support can help a person to think about problems in a different way, and this is emotion-focusing. ✓$\frac{1}{2}$ **(AO1 half)** However, it can be difficult to talk to someone you don't know, and support from close friends or family might be better. ✓$\frac{1}{2}$ **(AO2 half)** Rational emotive therapy teaches the person to think more positively about difficulties, and this can also be a good emotion-focusing strategy. ✓ **(AO1)** However, it is difficult to change thoughts and feelings. ✓$\frac{1}{2}$ **(AO2 half)** Defence mechanisms, such as denying that the situation is happening, may be a useful strategy. ✓ **(AO1)** In some situations, problem-focusing might be better, where practical steps are taken to alleviate the situation. ✓ **(AO2)** Women tend to use emotion-focusing more than men. ✓$\frac{1}{2}$ **(AO1 half)**

e **Some of the points are not fully explained, so half marks are given. If quite a good point is made, but not enough for a mark, and then another reasonable point is made, then 1 mark may be given for the two points. This essay shows some good examples of this. All 4 AO1 marks are given for some good, clear information about what emotion-focusing is. 2 AO2 marks are given, but two more points need to be made. A comment saying that emotion-focused and problem-focused strategies are often used together would have gained a further AO2 mark — for example, when taking direct action by doing something practical and changing thinking too. It could also be said that some problems are better dealt with by emotion-focusing, for example when something happens that cannot be changed in a practical sense. There is good communication and the answer is quite**

thorough, so 2 balance/breadth and 2 clarity/communication marks are given. This essay scores 10 marks out of 12.

(d) Coping strategies take more than one form and some are more effective than others. Focusing on the problem is not very useful if the problem cannot be changed. ✓ However, changing the situation, if possible, can be a good way of overcoming stress, and this is a problem-focused strategy. ✓ Some people focus on the emotion involved, for example by changing the way they look at the problem, and this can be useful. ✓ Counselling can help to focus on positive aspects or at least help individuals to blame themselves less. ✓ Defence mechanisms are sometimes used, such as denial or repression. This can work but can be destructive too, as energy is needed to keep thoughts unconscious and this energy could be used elsewhere. ✓

5 of a possible 6 marks are gained. This is quite a good discussion covering three types of coping. Each point is an assessment of the usefulness and so marks are gained each time. Elaboration of points shows understanding. The final mark could have been gained by discussing the use of more than one coping strategy at a time, and how that can be useful. Alternatively a comment about studies or methods used would have gained marks — for example, saying that defence mechanisms cannot really be tested so it is not proven that such mechanisms exist.

(e) Social resources, in particular social support, are important in coping with stress. ✓ For example, being without a job can be a stressful situation and unemployed people tend to cope better when they have support from others. It might be that social support helps directly, which is the direct effect hypothesis. This implies that lack of social support itself causes stress. ✓ However, it might be that social support simply helps; this is the stress buffering hypothesis. Either way, social support is important in alleviating (or not causing) stress. ✓ Another resource is personality type and cognitive factors. Competitive and self-critical people are type A. They will not cope with stressful situations as well as type B personalities, who are less hostile and less competitive. ✓ Cognitive strategies could help type A people to cope by considering their personality, and cognitive strategies would be a resource for coping. ✓ Type B people might need different cognitive strategies from type A people.

The 3 marks for the first resource are easily gained. The second resource is a bit unclear, as personality is not so much a resource as a causing factor. However, the idea that cognitive resources can make a difference is credited, as well as the explanation that different personality types might need different cognitive strategies. A further mark could have been gained if it were a bit clearer — for example, showing how type A people would need to focus more on realistic thinking (e.g. not having unrealistic work goals) than type B people, who are less competitive.

■ ■ ■

Question 3: Health promotion

(a) Based on the health belief model, explain what advice you would give to an Area Health Authority planning a health promotion campaign intended to reduce smoking in young people. (5 marks)

(b) Outline the basic features of the theory of reasoned action. (3 marks)

(c) Evaluate the theory of reasoned action in the context of health behaviour. (7 marks)

(d) Define the term primary prevention. (2 marks)

(e) Evaluate the use of primary prevention as a means for improving health. (4 marks)

e **(a)** All the marks here are for advice. This should be based on research. Say what the research shows and then say what advice you would therefore give.

(b) The 3 marks are for describing the theory of reasoned action. If a diagram is suitable as an answer, as could be the case for this question, then it is a good idea to include one. However, you will not get full marks for just a diagram. You need to explain the diagram or have clear sentences labelling it to achieve full marks.

(c) All 7 marks are for evaluation and comment. If you describe another theory briefly to make an evaluation point about the theory of reasoned action, then this is a good way of getting marks.

(d) You need to give a definition, but must write enough to get 2 marks. An example could be useful as elaboration.

(e) You need to say where primary prevention is useful and perhaps where it is not. Make two evaluative points and give examples or say more to elaborate on those points.

Answers to question 3

(a) The Area Health Authority could use shock tactics to show young people the dangers of smoking. The health belief model suggests that young people won't believe smoking will harm them or they won't think it will be that bad. ✓ Films and advertisements, like the recent one showing what happens to arteries, can show young people the effects and they might then link smoking to health issues and believe it could happen to them. ✓ They might also believe that the consequences would be severe. ✓ Then the AHA needs to show that stopping smoking can work and that it is not too late. ✓ It could do this by advertising. People who have given up smoking could say how much healthier they feel. ✓

e All 5 marks are awarded. The answer gives advice, as required, and links well to the model. There are two main areas in this answer. One considers changing young people's beliefs about the severity of the consequences; the other considers showing them that there is something they can do. These are the two areas of the model and make this a good answer.

(b) The theory of reasoned action (TRA) is similar to the health belief model but it includes the idea of norms and how we judge situations by considering the attitudes of others. ✓ People's health-related behaviour is used to judge their intentions. The idea is that we base our behaviour on a belief about what will happen and how successful our actions will be (in overcoming a health problem or preventing one) ✓ and that other people's responses to that behaviour are important too. ✓

e This is quite a good outline and 3 marks are achieved.

(c) The theory of reasoned action is good in that it adds the important aspect of social acceptability to the ideas of the health belief model. ✓

e This is a good point, but not enough to get more than 1 mark. The answer could be expanded by giving an example of social norms, such as when smoking is acceptable and modelled by media personalities compared with when it is not. Other evaluation points could be made — for example, saying that intentions do not always predict behaviour as the theory suggests. This point could be expanded by showing how many people actually want to give up smoking but do not do so. A further point that could be made is that people's past experiences will govern their behaviour as much as what other people think and this is not mentioned in the theory.

(d) Primary prevention is taking action to avoid any health problem in the first place, ✓ such as wearing a seat belt or having injections. ✓

e This is fine for 2 marks. The examples help to score the second mark.

(e) Primary prevention is useful if it prevents problems from occurring in the first place. Immunisation programmes have proved to be successful. ✓ There are problems in getting people to take action in this way, as they may not believe that anything will happen to them. ✓ However, when primary prevention measures are taken, then this can obviously help to avoid health problems in the first place, which is clearly beneficial to individuals and to society. ✓

e 3 marks are awarded. The last point could have been expanded for the fourth mark — it could be said that society benefits in terms of reduced costs as well as the health of the workforce.